Business Guides on the Go

"Business Guides on the Go" presents cutting-edge insights from practice on particular topics within the fields of business, management, and finance. Written by practitioners and experts in a concise and accessible form the series provides professionals with a general understanding and a first practical approach to latest developments in business strategy, leadership, operations, HR management, innovation and technology management, marketing or digitalization. Students of business administration or management will also benefit from these practical guides for their future occupation/careers.
These Guides suit the needs of today's fast reader.

Cordelia Friesendorf • Alena Blütener

Decentralized Finance (DeFi)

How Decentralized Applications (dApps) Disrupt Banking

Springer

Cordelia Friesendorf
SRH
Hamburg, Germany

Alena Blütener
Deloitte GmbH
Hamburg, Germany

ISSN 2731-4758 ISSN 2731-4766 (electronic)
Business Guides on the Go
ISBN 978-3-031-37487-6 ISBN 978-3-031-37488-3 (eBook)
https://doi.org/10.1007/978-3-031-37488-3

This Springer imprint is published by the registered company Springer Nature Switzerland AG
The registered company address is: Gewerbestrasse 11, 6330 Cham, Switzerland

Abstract

This book explores the possibility of decentralized finance (DeFi) disrupting traditional centralized finance in the near future. Decentralized finance is not a company or a single product in itself; instead, decentralized finance houses multiple products or services that act as a replacement for traditional centralized institutions such as insurance companies, banks, money markets, or bonds. These services are provided under so-called Decentralized Applications (dApps), which are mainly deployed via the Ethereum ecosystem. However, for dApps to process transactions, smart contracts are needed to lock in the required asset. These smart contracts are also self-executing. Therefore, DeFi carries much potential to eliminate intermediaries such as third-party financial providers. Consequently, there are multiple opportunities for DeFi to improve the financial industry and offer the stakeholder benefits such as a faster transaction time and an increase in control over their own assets. This book provides an in-depth analysis of the real-world use cases for DeFi, the Decentralized Ledger Technology (DLT), and digital assets, as well as their potential risks for financial institutions and consumers. We employ an online survey to understand consumer behavior and identify potential future trends in digital asset production and management. Digital assets are no longer only a choice for young and fearless investors but also hold the potential for attracting traditional investors from older generations. Decentralized finance is a promising approach to disrupt traditional centralized banking. Notwithstanding this, the DeFi space is still young and characteristically premature. This demonstrates several vulnerabilities for the predominant reasons such as liquidity mismatches, lack of shock-absorbing capacity, high leverage, and built-in interconnectedness. For DeFi to become a widely used intermediate for financial transactions, it must meet and satisfy several conditions, for example, adequate regulation or improved scalability of tokenization and blockchain.

Contents

Chapter 1
Decentralized Finance: How dApps Disrupt Banking

1.1 Loss of Trust in Banking

Defining Trust
Guiso (2010) defines trust as "the belief that an opponent in a relationship behaves accordingly to what he promised and does not take advantage of the person he is trading with. In other words, it is the probability that person A trading with B attaches to the possibility that B will behave opportunistically and take advantage of him. Trust is thus A's probability that B will not "cheat"."

Banks are without doubt one of the most important players in the development of the global monetary system over the past few decades, with a huge role to play in the process (Friesendorf & Stern, 2020; Friesendorf & Mir Haschemi, 2023). Moreover, they have made a significant contribution to society as a whole. It is believed that the first prototype banks of merchants in the ancient world made grain loans to farmers and traders transporting goods between cities in approximately 2000 BC within the Assyrian and Babylonian Empires. In the ancient Greek world as well as during the Roman Empire, lenders based in temples made loans and became adept at adding two important innovations to the loan process. The first was the acceptance of deposits, and the second was money changing. The discovery of money-lending activity has also been confirmed by archaeological evidence from this period in ancient China and India. By offering these services, temples became important financial hubs for the community, providing access to credit and a place to store and exchange money.

C. Friesendorf, A. Blütener, *Decentralized Finance (DeFi)*, Business Guides on the Go, https://doi.org/10.1007/978-3-031-37488-3_1

Functions of Money

- A measure of value
- Aids storage of value
- Legal tender
- A standard of deferred payment

As early as the Roman Empire, well-off Romans in ancient Rome kept their valuable possessions, such as jewelry and coins, in the basements of temples, believing them safe as the priests and workers were reverent and honest (Labate, 2016). In other words, articles or objects of value, or measures and embodiments of wealth would only be handed over under conditions of trust, to those worthy of trust in the community, such as the temples and the temple-keepers.

Historically speaking, the roots of banking in the modern sense of the word can be traced to the rich cities in the north like Florence, Venice, and Genoa. These cities were in the middle of medieval and early Renaissance Italy. At the turn of the fourteenth century, the Bardi and Peruzzi families dominated Florence's banking profession. They had set up branches throughout Europe in addition to their home base in Florence. They operated as rudimentary forms of banks, providing loans and other services to the wealthy merchants and nobility of the time. The success of these banks laid the foundation for the development of the banking system as we know it today.

The development of banking also spread throughout Europe over the course of the sixteenth and seventeenth centuries. This is due to several major innovations taking place in Amsterdam during the Dutch Republic, and in London during the seventeenth century. For example, the Amsterdamsche Wisselbank (the Bank of Amsterdam) was established in 1609, and it allowed individuals to deposit money or bullion and withdraw the money or the worth of the bullion, and it also required all bills of 600 gulden or upward to be paid through the bank.

A major change in the way banks operate because of advances in telecommunications and computer technology occurred during the twentieth century. This led to a dramatic increase in the size and geographical spread of banks as a result of these developments. For instance, the Internet and mobile banking have made it easier for customers to access banking services from different parts of the world. Many bank failures, including some of the largest banks in late 2000, are evidence seemingly dysfunctional systems that accumulate power and influence to the neglect of the customers at stake (Friesendorf & Uedelhoven, 2021). There was a resemblance between this phenomenon and that of the early years of the twentieth century. During the 1930s, an average of 9000 banks failed each year, with 4000 of those failures happening in 1933 alone.

Notwithstanding these events, over the years, banks have become an integral part of our everyday lives. People have trusted and relied on these institutions with their money and with their financial decisions ever since. Nevertheless, as pointed above, since the financial crisis of 2008, trust in these institutions has been greatly undermined.

The importance of trust in an economic system can be attributed to the fact that it is linked to the stability of financial markets. Furthermore, it is safe to write that the fact that trust prevails implies that the business model of financial institutions is a viable one. Generally, trust can be described as a quality or characteristic that provides the certainty that a transaction can be conducted successfully, no matter what knowledge or experience the transacting parties have about one another or whether they have prior experience with one another. Trust can also be defined as a quality or characteristic that guarantees the success of a transaction. Furthermore, trust allows the parties to the transaction to place their faith in the outcome, knowing that they will be rewarded with a successful outcome. It can be argued that trust is one of the most crucial factors in an economy that is built on the foundation of rationality-based transactionalism.

We can extend the principle of trust to argue that, in the absence of trust, people will not be willing to use the financial system. This can result in instability in the financial markets. If this happens, the demand for financial services can decrease, because of which monetary institutions might find it harder to remain profitable in the future. The lack of trust in the banking sector may have a detrimental effect on the economy, affecting the funding of private and public organizations and thereby impacting growth in output and employment. In other words, possible consequences of the lack of trust could mean the stagnation of economic growth accompanied by deflation. We can safely conclude that trust—as a key component of any economic system—is a crucial aspect influencing and determining the performance of an economy.

The stability of the financial system of an economy may be understood as an indication that there is a sufficient level of trust between the parties transacting within the system. On top of this, financial institutions such as banking, insurance, and pension funds produce or create trust in their performance-oriented functioning, turning them into a safe haven of transactional value storage for all transacting entities, be it individuals or businesses. It is also noted by Chernykh et al. (2019) that financial stability and trust have a strong relationship in terms of interdependency.

A fall in financial stability can also be seen as an erosion of trust between people (Guiso, 2010). A loss of trust in a financial system could result in a bank run in the worst-case scenario. There is also the possibility that low levels of trust could harm the financial services industry as well. Consumers who do not trust the industry will inevitably choose to engage less with it, which, in turn, will negatively impact both the industry and the economy, because of a reduction in the availability of capital for productive uses (Jaffer et al., 2014). In addition, consumers may switch to nonfinancial suppliers of financial services, such as technology companies and peer-to-peer markets.

Guiso (2010) argued that the collapse in trust played a crucial role in the global financial crisis as it led those who had developed distrust before the crisis to run on their banks as a result of the breakdown in trust. As a result, the role played by the plunge in confidence in the ability of financial institutions and their ability to repay their obligations is distinct from the role played by the decline in confidence about the solvency of financial institutions—the other factor that froze up financial markets and prompted investors to flee from them.

It was actually the revelation of the opportunistic behavior of some of the staff, which caused the collapse in trust to occur. The unfolding of the financial crisis brought to light by the Bernard Madoff fraud has been emblematic of the ensuing crisis. This has contributed to the entire financial industry being shrouded in darkness as a result of this scandal. It has been reported by Guiso (2010) that people who have lost faith in their bank are more than four times more likely than those who have retained full trust in the bank to run on it.

Bank Run
A bank run is a situation in which a large number of customers of a bank withdraw their deposits simultaneously due to concerns about the bank's solvency.

It is also relevant to point out that the global financial crisis has highlighted the excessive risk-taking behavior and shortcomings of banks and the traditional financial industry, which have exposed the need for a change in the system to be established. For years, banks have been endeavoring to restore the trust and confidence of their clients by enforcing new guidelines and rules, as well as focusing on good compliance practices in order to restore client trust and confidence.

For the public to be able to have confidence in individual banks, the financial stability of the entire industry is a sine qua non. Banks are interconnected, and the failure of one could potentially lead to a domino effect that could destabilize the whole industry. Therefore, having a strong financial system is essential for protecting customers and ensuring trust in the banking system. Sapienza and Zingales (2012) found that individuals who are highly trusting of banks and bankers are less likely to withdraw deposits and store them as cash because they fear that the bank's health will collapse if they withdraw deposits.

Trust has been mentioned by a number of researchers as a critical component of a successful financial sector, as it is vital to its proper functioning. A study by Harrison (2003: 206–07) views financial services as one of the most intangible types of services. Therefore, they can be difficult to understand because they are often complex and ambiguous. Despite pronounced information asymmetries, users of many products rely heavily on credibility qualities in order to determine their reliability, which places greater emphasis on the value of professional advice.

Despite the fact that many financial products are perceived to be risky, there is still a high level of perceived risk around their purchase. In a financial services marketing exchange, essentially, the customer is buying a set of promises from the company. As part of the purchase agreement, the financial institution promises to look after the buyer's funds and to ensure that their financial welfare is taken care of. Consequently, trust can be defined as a generalized expectation about how a financial institution will behave in the future based on the past. It is possible to derive generalized expectations of behavior from beliefs about acceptable behavior or norms, as well as from previous experiences with the bank or financial institution.

Several studies have been conducted to support the above points, with the conclusion being that as uncertainty increases, customers need to be able to rely on a product in order for it to be viable in their eyes. In that sense, financial professionals are valuable simply because of the trust they embody, especially in the areas of savings and investments, tax planning, insurance, mortgages or loans, and financial counseling.

Given the above arguments highlighting the need and value of trust, we can now look at how trust currently fares in a strongly innovation-oriented global-expansion-focused economic trajectory across the world. The latest trust barometer from Edelman—which is a survey that is conducted annually across 27 countries—shows there is a significant level of distrust among the population regarding the financial and banking sector as a whole. In some respects, the study indicates that there is a concerning trend in the financial services industry that needs to be addressed. In the months of May 2020 and January 2021, consumers' confidence in the finance sector plummeted by ten points, while their confidence in business in general has increased as a result of overcoming the Covid-19 pandemic. If banks and insurance companies wish to maintain customer loyalty, it is imperative that they rebuild customer confidence as quickly as possible.

It is not uncommon for financial services leaders to speak about trust, and companies often place customer trust at the forefront of their corporate strategy and an integral aspect of their unique selling proposition. The importance of gaining the trust of your customers cannot be overstated. There is an important difference between these terms, despite the fact that they sound similar at first glance. There is a generalized expectation that someone will be reliable as we have discussed above, which is what trust refers to. As a result, confidence facilitates the development of trust between parties. It is evident from the Edelman study that there is a deficit in customer confidence, and with that comes a lack of trust among customers.

Taking a closer look at the lack of trust in the business raises deeper problems in the minds of customers. In recent years, there seems to be a deterioration in the value of what is offered by financial institutions. Due to the advancement of technology and innovation, customer expectations are increasingly focused on receiving an exciting customer experience rather than the basic function of using financial products as a safe haven for excess funds. The financial industry looks to solutions in the areas of customizing customer needs that enhance their daily quality of life, especially given new crises such as the pandemic that has impacted their personal and working life.

This report has sparked a general consensus among financial institutions that they should change their approach to strategy and operational culture, which involves rewording their products and rebranding them with a focus on how the customers perceive the products. In this way, customization has become the means to adapt the product in a way that allows it to be more like a consumer good in terms of enabling an exciting customer journey. The traditional view of finance products as safe havens was clearly shifted.

Corona pandemic left a lasting impression on many people when a continuous reassessment of how life was being lived, how money was being spent, and how different activities were valued in a changed environment was unavoidable as a result of the pandemic. The result of this is that customers are not thinking in terms of consumption versus savings when it comes to spending. As a consequence of the Corona pandemic, customer spending has changed and priorities have been reversed, causing health to be ranked as a top priority. As we move forward in the years to come, it is safe to say that consumer behavior patterns, preferences, and perceptions are becoming increasingly influenced by their financial situations. In such a new and ever-changing environment, banks and other financial institutions are being asked to provide customers with services that they may not have previously been able to get. Investors are also becoming increasingly aware of the importance of making financial decisions based on their core values, such as assessing the sustainability, climate change initiatives, social welfare goals, diversity, and fairness credentials of financial institutions, before making a financial commitment.

Overall, there is much change taking place in the financial industry, which is to a large extent caused by the falling trust. As of now, the only industry that has a lower trust rating than the financial services industry is the media, and since 2008, the banking industry in all countries has only been able to gain very few points in total. Moreover, it has been found that the countries with the highest level of distrust against the banking industry are primarily European nations, such as France, Spain, Germany, Italy, Ireland, and the United Kingdom. It is interesting to note that on the other hand, India holds the most trust among the countries when it comes to banking and finance (Edelman 2021a, b). In the next sections, we explore how falling trust in the financial industry is creating room for innovation to transform the traditional playground of finance.

1.1.1 Rethink and Innovation

For institutionalized banking to become more trustworthy in the future, there needs to be a rethink and innovation in the sector and a focus less on compliance and more on benevolence. Because of the lack of trust in the banking system, many economic stakeholders from households to big and small businesses have been exploring ways to come up with their own alternatives to traditional banking as a result of the lack of trust. This is where the concept of decentralized finance comes into play.

Additionally, despite the fact that globalization and digitalization are bringing about a rise in the sharing of personal data between banks and their customers, studies have shown that customers are more willing to do so if they can recoup their investments due to the benefits they receive from such sharing. There is no question about the fact that transactional thinking or transactionalism is essential to the evolution of customer journeys in which customers expect honesty, transparency, information provision, security and protection of their accounts and transactions to be key priorities in financial activities.

In the last few years, rich and fascinating customer experiences coupled with data privacy or digital trust have become key components of financial products, whether it be banking, asset management, insurance, or pension funds. In order for any of these to be achieved, information is required to be of good or high quality. In other words, data cleansing to reduce inaccurate information is the need of the day. It is generally agreed that the financial industry is substantially influenced by the high levels of customer mobility as well as the trends of innovation in the industry. Moreover, sustainability and social goals are becoming increasingly important in product architecture.

Decentralized finance, or DeFi as it is known, is one of the fastest-growing sectors that has sprung up around cryptocurrencies and blockchains in recent years. Basically, the idea behind decentralized finance is to create a global and decentralized economy that combines all existing financial services that are currently centralized into one global community. It is the goal of decentralized finance to create a more equitable economic system, such as through the use of blockchain technology and the Internet (CoinGecko Lau et al. 2020). Blockchain technology and the Internet are critical infrastructure that make the theoretical option of decentralized finance a reality.

Decentralized Finance (DeFi in Short)

DeFi is a young concept of a monetary system that aims to remove middlemen and/or diverse financial intermediaries in the traditional banking system by using innovation and technology solutions to create a global financial landscape that connects borrowers and lenders directly catering to the goals of value and convenience.

Accessibility, centralization, and transparency are expected to be the pillars of such a system. These are expected to create a monetary landscape that builds on trust in technology and direct interaction of stakeholders, without a middleman such as the bank, as we know it today.

1.1.2 Democratization of Global Banking

Specifically, DeFi seeks to improve three key segments that are currently found within the traditional banking system in order to make it more reliable. Accessibility, centralization, and transparency, as well as the payment and clearance systems, are some of the aspects that are important. It is projected that decentralized finance will be able to connect and bring financial services to 1.7 billion unbanked people in the world (CoinGecko Lau et al., 2020) and thus enable them to participate fully in the global economic system. It is also noteworthy that decentralized finance has the advantage of not being censored by any government agencies or banks as it utilizes stablecoins and automated protocols, including smart contracts, to facilitate the transfer of funds (Aramonte et al., 2021). As a result, decentralized finance operates without censorship and eliminates middlemen like banks and intermediaries from the process.

There are, however, a number of regulatory challenges, risks, and concerns regarding the safety of decentralized finance which need to be addressed. As a result of liquidity mismatches, a lack of shock-absorbing capacity, high leverage, and built-in interconnectedness, the DeFi space is still premature, showing several vulnerabilities due to a lack of shock-absorbing capacity, among other factors. DeFi would need to satisfy several conditions in order to become one of the most widely used intermediaries for financial transactions in the future, such as proper regulation and improved scalability for tokenization and blockchains (see Aramonte et al., 2021).

Our objective in this book is to conduct an investigation into whether decentralized finance is capable of disrupting or derailing institutions such as banks and how this may occur. We elaborate on the plan of the book in the following section.

1.1.3 Motivation and Plan of the Book

One of the main objectives of this book is to critically analyze the existing banking sector both at the global level and at the local level in various countries. Aims are to verify and compare measures of change that have taken place in this very traditional industry, both in the context of the international economy and within the borders of Germany and the rest of Europe in general. We intend to provide an overview of centralized finance in this chapter. We will look at the history of banks and their competitors, as well as provide a guide on how a bank can obtain the necessary licenses to conduct business.

As a part of Chap. 2, we will discuss the concept of decentralized finance, along with the technology that enables it. The purpose of Chap. 3 is to prepare the reader on the different categories of decentralized finance that are available today, such as decentralized payments, decentralized derivatives, lotteries, loans, borrowings, and exchanging with decentralized financing. The main focus of our research is to determine the advantages and disadvantages of decentralized finance over centralized finance, as well as demonstrate potential real-world use cases that can be applied to decentralized finance.

The purpose of Chap. 4 is to compare and contrast centralized finance with decentralized finance. It should also be noted that, as you can expect with new technology, there is always a risk and a security concern associated with it, which we will discuss and analyze in this thesis. The objective of Chap. 5 is to carry out an empirical analysis through the use of an online survey to customers to determine the potential of decentralized finance by means of empirical analysis. Our focus here is on the satisfaction of current customers with traditional centralized banks, the use of digital assets, and their investment behavior. In Chap. 6, we will provide a comprehensive analysis of the status quo and future trends in the world economy in terms of decentralized finance. The outcomes of the online survey will further be analyzed based on the results of the survey to determine whether, in the near future, decentralized finance will be able to disrupt traditional centralized banking or not.

There is a detailed discussion in Chap. 7 concerning the ways in which strategic agility can help traditional banks regain their power and the trust of their clients in the future. In addition, we summarize the insights, learnings, and results that are likely to be of benefit to banks, financial institutions, central banks, policy-makers, start-ups, and private investors.

References

Aramonte, S., Huang, W., & Schrimpf, A. (2021). DeFi risks and the decentralisation illusion. *BIS Quarterly Review*, Bank for International Settlements, December.

Chernykh, L., Davydov, D., & Sihvonen, J. (2019). *Financial stability and public confidence in banks*. BOFIT Discussion Papers 2.

CoinGecko Lau, D., Lau, D., Jin, T. S., Kho, K., Azmi, E., Lee, T., & Ong, B. (2020). *How to DeFi: Beginner* (1st ed.). Independently Published.

Edelman. (2021a). *Edelman Trust Barometer 2021*. In Edelman Barometer. https://www.edelman.com/sites/g/files/aatuss191/files/2021-03/2021 Edelman Trust Barometer.pdf

Edelman. (2021b). *Edelman Trust Barometer 2021 Technology Sector*. Edelman. https://www.edelman.com/sites/g/files/aatuss191/files/2021-03/2021 Edelman Trust Barometer Tech Sector Report_0.pdf

Friesendorf, C., & Stern, J. (2020). Mangelnde Digitalisierung in der Finanzbranche. In *Digitalisierung des Auslandszahlungsverkehrs. essentials*. Springer. https://doi.org/10.1007/978-3-658-32738-5_1

Friesendorf, C., & Uedelhoven, L. (2021). Digital transformation of global mobility markets. In *Mobility in Germany. Springer briefs in business*. Springer. https://doi.org/10.1007/978-3-030-71849-7_1

Friesendorf, C., & Mir Haschemi, N. J. (2023). Private equity in Germany. In *Venture Capital for Digital Platform Start-ups. Springer business guides on the go*. Springer. https://doi.org/10.1007/978-3-031-33708-6

Guiso, L. (2010). *A trust-driven financial crisis. Implications for the future of financial markets*. EUI Working paper ECO2010/07.

Harrison, T. (2003). Why trust is important in customer relationships and how to achieve it. *Journal of Financial Services Marketing, 7*(3), 206–209.

Jaffer, S., Morris, N., & Vines, D. (2014). Why trustworthiness is important. In N. Morris & D. Vines (Eds.), *Capital failure: Rebuilding trust in financial services*. Oxford University Press.

Labate, V. (2016). *Banking in the roman world - World history encyclopedia*. World History Encyclopedia. https://www.worldhistory.org/article/974/banking-in-the-roman-world/.

Sapienza, P., & Zingales, L. (2012). A trust crisis. *International Review of Finance, 12*(2), 123–131.

Chapter 2
Centralized Finance

2.1 The Evolution of Banking in Europe

Banking has existed since the beginning of time when the first currencies were created. The idea of a bank came about when empires had to find a way to pay for goods and services that were purchased from foreign suppliers when they needed to buy them. As an alternative to paying with farm animals, coins were made from a variety of metals for easier and more convenient transactions. As a result, it was extremely important to find a way of storing the precious metals and keeping them safe from burglars and other intruders who might try to steal them. There was no safe place to store wealth for most ancient families in the early ages of mankind, so people kept their coins in temples in the early ages of mankind, where they trusted good priests and honest workers with their valuables in order to keep their wealth safe. Moreover, ancient records from Rome, Greece, and Egypt prove that temples acted not only as storage facilities for money but as lending institutions as well (Labate, 2016).

Literature shows that there is a strong connection between the history of banking and that of money, but the history of banking transactions is probably much older than the invention of money. In the early days, deposits were mainly grain, but later on, they included cattle, agricultural implements, and precious metals such as gold, in the form of easy-to-transport compressed plates, as well as other goods, including gold, silver, and other precious metals. It should be noted that the economic life of the people originally revolved around the houses of the familiaregala, along with their priestly order, where security was provided for storage and distribution as well as for the distribution of food in the past before the establishment of Christianity. It is thus the buildings that were primarily used by this elite group, the palaces and temples, that became the location for the earliest of social exchange practices bearing some similarities to the banking practices of the present-day culture, wherein the safeguarding of the wealth of the community was ensured. There was no doubt that temples and palaces were the safest places to keep gold since they were constantly tended and well maintained.

C. Friesendorf, A. Blütener, *Decentralized Finance (DeFi)*, Business Guides on the Go, https://doi.org/10.1007/978-3-031-37488-3_2

2.2 Trust as a Store of Value

It is crucial that we understand these humble origins of banking in order to uncover the most important asset that any bank can have: trust (Friesendorf & Stern, 2020; Friesendorf & Mir Haschemi, 2023). As a double ownership scheme, trust was institutionalized by goldsmiths in the early seventeenth century when they institutionalized the double ownership scheme (Kim, 2011). Due to its limited supply, chemical stability, cost density, and size (a small coin could pay for a lot of goods), gold was regarded as a universally accepted currency throughout the world. There was a time when goldsmiths were trusted to verify the purity of gold as well as to rate it and to safeguard it, an attitude that was similar to that of those who stored their valuables in temples during the Roman Empire. It was the reputation and the trust of their clients that fueled the business model of the goldsmiths. The goldsmith's facilities had to be fortified and protected due to the value of the materials, which made the goldsmith an ideal place to store gold due to the fact that this was a reliable and safe method of storage. To store their gold in the safe kept by the goldsmith, people had to pay a fee to the goldsmith for this service. In exchange, the goldsmith gave them a deposit receipt, which provided peace of mind for the people and another source of income for the goldsmith (Kim, 2011). As you can see, this process is quite similar to that used by traditional banks today, which offer negative interest rates on deposits.

Goldsmiths were able to lend out a greater amount of gold than they actually had in their vaults by taking advantage of the commodification of trust by issuing deposit receipts that could be used directly to transact with other people. Thus, in this way, the goldsmith was even able to receive interest on gold that he did not have at the time, and the person that had the receipt could still use the receipt to pay. As a result, many people believed that they could get their gold back in exchange for the receipt, which is a win–win situation for all parties involved in the transaction. When a person is unable to withdraw his gold from the goldsmith's vault, and the goldsmith does not have the amount of gold listed on the receipt, the word would spread quickly, and several people would immediately return the receipts to try to retrieve their gold, and the goldsmith would go bankrupt if the goldsmith did not have the gold that was on the receipt. Because of the inherent nature of this system, it relied on people rarely resorting to a withdrawal of their resources as a result. Consequently, there was no bank run, thereby locking in the interests of the customers (Kim, 2011).

2.3 The Institutionalization of Trust

Throughout the years, the goldsmith system became more institutionalized, and goldsmiths became bankers, which are the main places today where money is lent and deposited. We also find evidence for an emergence of the goldsmith system as an accepted and trusted method of preserving value such that it became mainstream across levels of income and wealth. It is because of the history of banking that it has resulted in the creation of the definition of a bank, which is an organization that holds other people's money, invests, and lends it in order to acquire more money or a building that houses the organization (Cambridge Dictionary, 2021).

2.4 Banking License Types

A company needs to comply with strict government regulations in order to operate as a bank, which is why it must obtain a so-called banking license to earn the credentials to function as a bank (Friesendorf & Uedelhoven, 2021). When a company holds this license, it is certified that it meets all the regulations and legal requirements in order to be able to protect the data and the money of its customers.

An individual or business can apply for a number of different types of bank licenses in Europe, including the following categories:

2.4.1 *E-Money Licenses*

This type of license is designed for companies that offer financial services and payments such as currency exchanges and transfers. It should be noted, however, that the company cannot operate as a bank or manage deposits as a result of its e-money license.

2.4.2 *Fintech License*

The company would have to apply for a Fintech license or a traditional license (BaFin, 2021a).

2.4.3 *Extended License*

It is possible for a fintech company that wishes to partner with a bank to obtain a license that is known as an extended license. By doing this, the business can be operated under the license of the parent bank (N26, 2020). It is possible to apply for a license when you wish to operate as a digital bank (only virtual), with a focus on the virtual customer experience, in order to operate as a fintech company (European Central Bank, 2019).

2.4.4 *Traditional License*

Last but not least, the traditional license can only be obtained by large cooperations that offer in-person services, operate on a larger scale, or have their own branch offices in banking institutions.

It is customary in Germany that any company that wishes to obtain a banking license must make an application to the Bundesanstalt für Finanzdienstleistungsaufsicht (BaFin), which then submits a proposal to the European Central Bank (ECB) for approval.

An illustration of such a process of obtaining a banking license can be found in Fig. 2.1.

2.5 Banking License Criteria

In order to assess the application, both the Banking Supervisory Board or Agency, namely in Germany, Bundesanstalt für Finanzdienstleistungsaufsicht (BaFin), and the European Central Bank (ECB) will consider different criteria such as the initial capital, the business plan, the requirements for managing directors, and the holders of qualifying holdings (BaFin, 2021b).

2.5.1 *Initial Capital*

The initial capital is the minimum amount of capital that a company is required to maintain throughout its existence in order to make it viable. In the case of credit institutions (such as banks), the minimum amount of capital required is five million

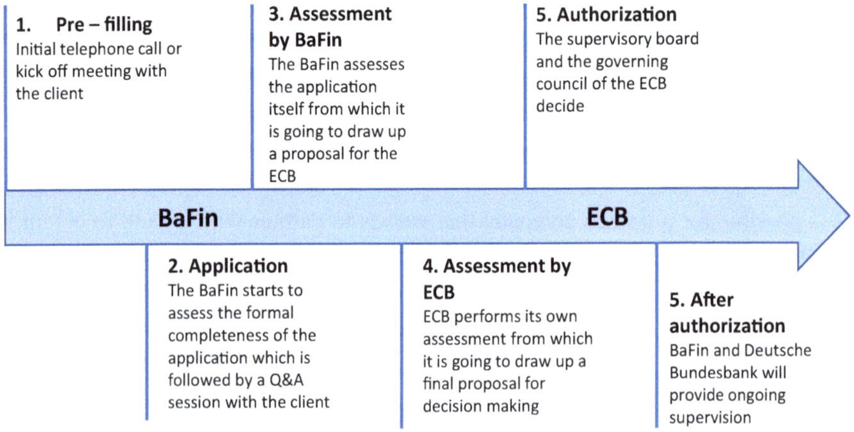

Fig. 2.1 Granting of authorization involving the European Central Bank, own illustration based on BaFin, 2021

euros (European Central Bank, 2019). As for the initial amount that a business is required to pay, it varies depending on the type of banking license they are seeking.

2.5.2 *Business Plan*

An important part of the application is the company's business plan, which provides a comprehensive view of the intention and purpose of the founding of the bank as well as details of the business model, including the products that the bank would offer. As part of the risk management process, the BaFin checks if the business plan is feasible and complies with the minimum requirements of risk management. Furthermore, the business plan should include information such as the organizational structure, the scope, and nature of the business, as well as the projected figures and a plan for the internal system to comply with the requirement of risk management (Bundesanstalt für Finanzdienstleistungsaufsicht, 2021).

2.5.3 *Requirements for Managing Directors*

Ideally, for a business to be able to apply for a banking license from the BaFin, it needs to have at least two suitable managing directors who are capable of performing their functions and who are able to observe the number of directorships held by the business. During the course of their professional career, a suitable managing director should have acquired sufficient knowledge as well as practical experience to be able to manage the bank as a firm that achieves profitability, productivity, liquidity, and value securing in the framework of the proposed business model (Merkblatt Zu Den Geschäftsleitern Gemäß KWG, ZAG Und KAGB, 2020).

2.5.4 *Requirements for the Holders of Qualifying Holdings*

In addition, the BaFin also takes a look at the size and composition of the disclosed holdings as well as the holders of those holdings. Any holding that represents 10% or more of the voting rights or capital of the company can be considered a qualifying holding. A further requirement is that the holders of the shares should also be suitable (proper and fit) and must meet the required conditions in order to ensure an effective and well-informed management of the business (Bundesanstalt für Finanzdienstleistungsaufsicht, 2021).

As a result of the successful assessment of the BaFin, the ECB will receive a proposal, conduct its own review, and prepare a proposal for the governing council and supervisory board that authorizes the ECB to issue a banking license to the company. It is nevertheless true that the BaFin will continue to observe and supervise the business even after it has been authorized. When it comes to significant institutions, the ECB will be directly responsible for supervising them and conducting observations that are of a monitoring nature in the interest of the customers of the bank as well as the overall stability of the banking system.

2.6 Bank Categories, Business Models, and Products

There are a wide range of ways in which an institution such as a bank operates, and it offers a spectrum of products tailored to the needs of the stakeholders specific to the sector and to the market as a whole. Therefore, more prominent financial institutions are often divided into different groups based on their type of operations. The operating or product divisions within a bank often differ. In principle, banks offer different kinds of banking. These are, namely, global banking, private banking or wealth management, investment banking, retail banking, and corporate banking. We describe the nature and characteristics of these kinds in the following subsections.

2.6.1 Global Banking

Global banks are a by-product of the increasing globalization and interconnectedness of economies. High mobility of labor, goods, services, and capital are prime reasons for the success and profitability of global banks, which are, in effect, business conglomerates that operate in home and host countries catering to the funding and transacting needs of local and international businesses of various sizes. Together with national banks, these global banks form the fundamental infrastructure of the global financial system and thereby represent a systemic risk as well as an opportunity.

With the increase in digitalization, e-commerce, and advanced technologies-based service solutions, it is becoming attractive and more common for larger corporations to move beyond their home markets, to transact cross-border, and to do business around the world. Global banks offer a variety of products and services to their customers, including foreign currency accounts and credit cards, transborder advisory services, and/or multicurrency management. Primarily global banks offer financial services to companies that are trading internationally and require currency denominations, leveraging, and factoring, among others.

They are also involved in foreign direct investment as well as cross-country portfolio investments. Specifically, in the fields of logistics such as shipping and aviation, public infrastructure projects involving telecommunication and technology networks, and pharmaceuticals, global banks are key stakeholders in providing operating finance internationally. The organizational structures, unique selling points as part of their business models, and the risk management strategies vary significantly. Global banks, despite their size, operate in a highly competitive market that is a boon to the customers, who are both corporates as well as households.

2.6.2 *Private Banking/Wealth Management*

Private banking or wealth management is one of the oldest forms of banking that involves special care given to the financial management needs of high net-worth individuals or families who can be characterized as private clients. A wide range of products and services are usually offered, such as insurance, loans, and investments. In Germany, private banking falls under the supervisory aegis of the German Banking Act, German Securities Trading Act, German Investment Act, and overall the German Civil Code. The monitoring authorities are the German national bank, i.e. the Bundesbank as well as the BaFin. Depending on the services provided, a minimum sum of 75,000 € is due for obtaining a license to operate, for example, as an advisory provider in the German market.

As compared to other forms of banking, private banking or wealth management is subject to close monitoring by the above-mentioned authorities to check for money laundering or elements of financial crime. This requires that private banks and wealth managers undertake organizational procedures and continuous due diligence that involve regular reporting and ensuring transparency in financial dealings to ensure rule-based functioning or risk the loss of the license, which typically ends up in financial losses such as a sanctioning of a fine of up to five million euros or 10% of the revenue of the bank. The worse consequence is often the reputational loss for the bank, which discourages potential clients from exploring business opportunities with the bank.

Private banking continues to be a growing sector catering to the needs of individuals that have at least one million euros in liquid assets. This growth can be attributed to socio-demographic factors such as an aging population, entrepreneurship that is retail and tech-driven, and highly interested in investment options with high rates of return with high risk tolerance, as well as a high concentration of wealth. There is a need today for sophisticated advice on financial investment that relies on the knowledge and know-how of relationship managers that address the clients' interests, including aspects of sustainability.

In particular, in this form of banking, trust plays a vital role since most of the marketing takes place by word of mouth. Success in private banking thereby relies on clarity, transparency, risk-reward proportions, and the overall performance of the portfolio. Despite the overall increase in regulation, private banking in Germany is today a very competitive field with much fluctuation of clients between leading players.

Digitalization is rapidly changing the traditional business model structure that relies on personal interaction and developing client affinity. Fee-only and online subscription models are slowly and steadily replacing the personal face-to-face business model. Simultaneously, hybrid advisory models are in high demand since they cater to the customer experience of highly mobile and digital clients today.

2.6.3 Investment Banking

An investment banking firm is devoted to assisting its customers with raising capital through various products and services, such as equity and debt issuances, mergers and acquisitions, investing in excess funds, and hedge investments, or by helping to launch an initial public offering. Clients can be entities, governments, or corporations. Investment banks help individuals and institutions in assessing the market for the launch of initial public offerings as well as executing these IPO transactions toward the successful launch of a corporation into the market. They are involved in mergers and acquisitions, leveraged buyouts, restructuring activities of companies such as divestitures, and leveraging securities, including brokerage. A primary function of investment banks is to provide financial advisory services and the function of underwriting.

The business model of an investment bank aims to trade and transact in capital and money markets on the one hand to gain wealth for themselves as well as to function as an agency for their clients. JP Morgan, Goldman Sachs, Bank of America Merrill Lynch, Citi, Morgan Stanley, Barclays, and Deutsche Bank are a few global leaders charging a fee for each transaction in a range between 7% to 17%. Investment banks have unique firm structures providing a spectrum of functions ranging from M&A advisory, trading, customized services, and equity research. Some of them also offer private wealth management services.

Despite the losses during the financial crisis of 2011 and the heavy criticism that followed, investment banking continues to be a product and service and high demand of global and domestic corporations as well as government financing needs. Investment banks contained a high level of systemic risk. At the same time, they are relevant and critical players or stakeholders in the functioning of the global financial system.

2.6.4 Retail/Consumer Banking

Specifically, the retail banking division consists of the products and services that are typically associated with the daily business of individuals, such as credit cards, mortgages, or the provision of savings and checking accounts (Majaski, 2021). Retail or consumer banks exist and thrive on personal relationships with customers due to the intimacy of personal finances. Consumer banking depends completely on customer trust. Landscape of retail or consumer finance is changing dramatically today with the entry of agile fintex that is cutting off long-established customers with spending and payment products. Big tech companies such as Google, Apple,

Amazon, and Alibaba offer interesting personal finance solutions while offering an engaging customer experience at a level that cannot be met by the traditional retail players in the local as well as in the global market.

These new digital products and services include payments, savings, borrowings, and investments, all offered in combination with discount or coupon systems that provide for a holistic banking experience that had no precedence. Traditional banks now face the challenge of keeping up with the high standards our benchmarks set by the new entrance, including fintechs, which offer a delightful solution. Customer experience is expected to provide ease of use, convenience, and a high sense of gratification. Specifically, younger customers are looking for banks that offer them agile solutions that also meet the goals of sustainability as stated by the United Nations.

Protection of biodiversity, climate change, and keeping a small carbon footprint are also features expected by young clients in consumer banking, besides new product solutions such as mobile apps, secure online banking platforms, digital wallets, and digital payment systems, as well as a host of tangible goods that come together as a benefit in the overall package of banking. Consumer banking does hold the promise of getting disrupted by new technologies as well as pioneering players in the market. Overall, the competition is extremely high in retail and consumer banking.

2.6.5 Corporate Banking

There is a great deal of similarity between the corporate banking division and the retail banking division. In spite of this, instead of focusing on individuals or smaller audiences, the corporate division is responsible for taking care of minor or more significant corporate clients, depending on their size. It is also important to note that the corporate banking division also offers advisory services, such as relationship management, to its clients (CFI, 2020).

Corporate banking caters to wholesale clients that include large corporations, financial institutions such as pension funds, governments, and other semi-government agencies or entities. The services offered by corporate divisions of banks include commercial banking such as deposit taking, lending, lines of credit, and the offering of a variety of financial transactions. This also includes the offer of international transactions that include currency obligations and managing against price fluctuations, investment banking, project finance for large infrastructure projects, or for the issuing of bonds as a syndicate, among others. Insurance, advisory services, and shareholding are additional services that are offered by corporate banks.

Corporate banking is not free of criticism. Several crises in the past across the global financial system show that many of these have been involved in speculative finances, such as Ponzi schemes that have resulted in bankruptcy. While the bailing has been carried out by national governments, corporate banks have been criticized for accumulating risk and often using complex and transparent systems of evaluation that enhance this risk. Due to the close working with government and or regulatory entities, there is suspicion that there could be conflicts of interest that are not comparable with the other kinds of banking, which makes corporate banking on the overall a risky and expensive venture. Corporate banking today faces high regulation, slower growth, an increase in competition, and an emergence of a digital legal system that has a substantial effect on costs and dampens revenue.

Depending on the type of activity that the bank is engaged in, they can also be classified as bulge bracket banks, middle-market banks, elite boutique banks, or industry banks. Here is a chart that illustrates the four main categories that are most prevalent in investment banking and some examples of key players who fit into each category.

A breakdown of banking categories can be found in Fig. 2.2.

2.6.6 *Bulge Brackets*

There are many large financial institutions that fall under the bulge brackets that offer a wide range of financial services, such as equity research, investment banking, consumer lending, and sales and trading services. There is a tendency for these

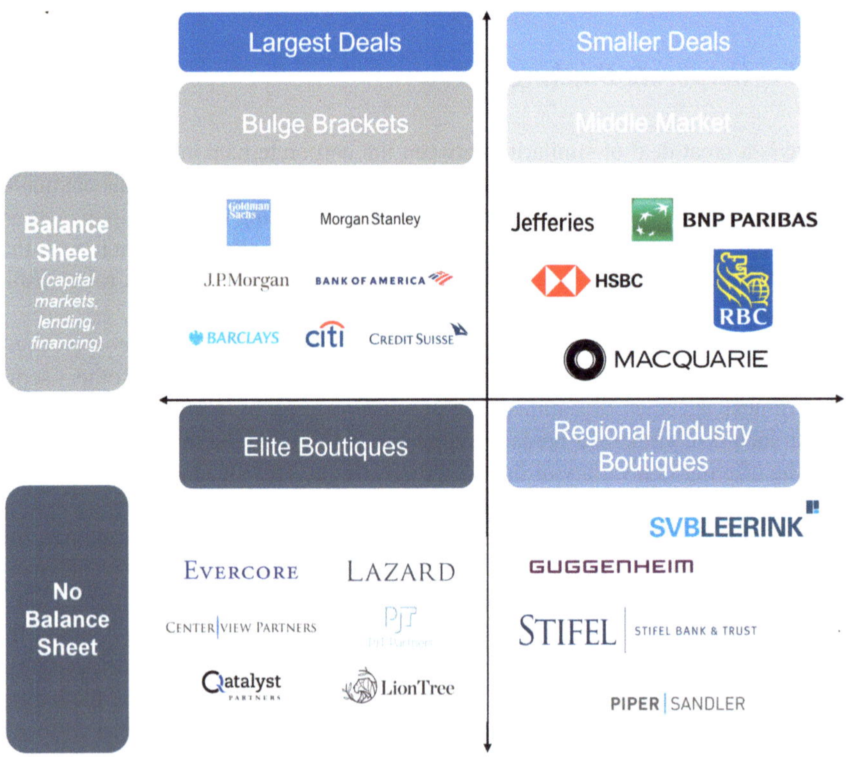

Fig. 2.2 Banking categories

institutions to have a long history of providing financial services and of being located in many different locations around the globe, which is why they tend to have the most prominent clients and to be involved in the most significant deals.

A bulge bracket bank is an institution that has a balance sheet, so it is considered a bank. This allows them to be able to provide their clients with more ease of securing financing as they are able to take on underwriting risk when they execute deals on behalf of their clients (Corporate Finance Institute, 2021a). Originally emerging in the late 90s, bulge bracket emerged as the investment bank's preparedness to accept any deal. Since the banks were listed in a sequential order based on the significance of their role in the deal, the top bracket of the banks was referred to as the "bulge."

The bulge bracket has thereby been in the lead in the launch of any new financial product. Dating back to history, during the launch of mortgage-backed securities, credit default swaps, or even carbon emission trading, bulge bracket banks were the first to participate and determine the outcome of the performance of the new financial products that were launched. Factors that need to be considered in the bulge bracket banks are notably capitalization, volume, applicability, acceptability, the spread of the product, and finally the reputation of the investment bank.

By nature of the structure of the business model, the ad hoc publicity, and the visibility in the market, make bulge brackets a source of status or of aspirational value in the eyes of market participants, especially investment bankers; therefore, there is a high level of competition to partner or collaborate with such blue-ribboned product market. On the negative side, the bulge bracket attracts controversies such as overvaluation and misleading market information.

2.6.7 Middle Market

There are several similarities between middle-market banks and bulge bracket banks; for example, they both have a balance sheet, offer a full range of financial services, and are globally well-established players in the financial industry. However, they tend to work with small or medium-sized companies that often have an enterprise value of less than 1 billion USD (Corporate Finance Institute, 2021b), which means they tend to deal with small or mid-sized companies.

Developments in this segment show that there is a high level of competition since banks aim to position themselves primarily on price since there is little room for product or service differentiation. Additionally, the impact of digitalization is increasing the dynamics of competition as the bank with the most attractive offer in terms of customer service eventually wins over the client. As a result, middle-market banks possess an intrinsic motivation to finetune their brand, offer, customer outreach, sales, and marketing approach and thereby determine their competitive positioning in the market.

Factors that drive middle-market banks are operational investment needs of small and medium-sized companies that require short or medium-term financing.

Asset-based and cash-flow financing are typical approaches to obtaining operational finance. The financing of mergers and acquisitions in hypercompetitive markets is also a need fulfilled by middle-market banks. Overall, middle-market banks enjoy a deep-rooted customer relationship that lasts in the worst case for a decade and in the best case across family generations, which is an important reason for their established stability in financial markets.

2.6.8 Elite Boutique

There is a distinction between elite boutique banks and bulge bracket or middle-market banks. The term “independent advisors” can be used to describe them. A boutique does not have a balance sheet, and it focuses more on pure financial advisory activities, such as restructurings and M&As, than on having a balance sheet.

Elite boutique banks build a strong contrast to the bulge bracket banks as they universally focus on generic financial advisory services or specialized niche research advice in financial management. The business model of elite boutiques is structured to cater to customized financial products and services to the needs, preferences, and budget limitations of their pool of clients. In size, they are thereby smaller and enjoy the advantage of the flexibility to adapt to client needs. Furthermore, elite boutique advisory banks offer services and merger and acquisition advisory, thereby accompanying the clients closely such that the partnership networks and an inherent client culture determine the unique advantages of this business model.

2.6.9 Regional or Industry Boutiques

A regional or industry boutique is identical to the structural form and client focus of an elite boutique, but the presence of this boutique is smaller, and its location is more restricted to a specific region or an industrial sector. It is for this reason that they work on a smaller scale than elite boutiques.

The financial institutes in each category compete against each other for clients, prestige, new talent, and deals, all of which will be discussed in more detail in the following section.

2.7 Banking Competition in Retail Markets

In the financial industry, there is a lot of competition between financial stakeholders, be it banking and nonbanking institutions, because of the intensification of the globalization of the world economy. Banks compete with each other more than they do with other businesses because of the nature of their business model. They are centralized institutions that provide financial services that function as intermediaries connecting governments, corporations, and individuals in an orderly fashion that caters to the savings and investment needs of each party. Banks offer a wide variety of products and services with the goal of contributing to the individual profitability, productivity, liquidity, and, in many cases, security needs of their customers.

Be it for households or businesses, big or small, these services can be in the form of capital funds or cash flows that cater to spending, investment, strategic financing, or operational funding of various activities in an economic unit. Because of these functions, banks enjoy an exclusive position in the macroeconomy. At the same time, banking performance builds on their ability to generate trust among old and new clients. This is also why they compete with other players in the financial industry for the expansion of a trust-based market share.

When it comes to the financial industry, banks used to be the most significant players. This is a situation that is so pertinent that the combined market capitalization of the top 10 banks combined is valued at over USD 2 trillion as of 2021, which is illustrated in Fig. 2.3. This figure demonstrates the market capitalization of the top 10 banks combined.

As inferred from the table above, two major bulge bracket US banks are leading the global market place, while being closely followed by the two largest Chinese banks: International Chinese Banking Corporation (ICBC) and China Merchants Bank.

When it comes to the German financial market, there are local or national key players that are influential. Figure 2.4 is a matrix that highlights the most significant financial service providers in Germany.

It can be seen from Fig. 2.4 that Deutsche Bank holds a dominant position in the market. In addition to offering advice to the most prominent companies in the German market, the bank has offices around the world. There were 1.348 billion dollars in revenue generated by Deutsche Bank in 2020, which is nearly three times as much as the second most successful bank in Germany, the DZ Bank, which generated 519 million euros in revenue. The financial landscape of Germany is

Rank	Name of Bank	Country	Market Capitalization in USD
1	JPMorgan Chase & Co	USA	466.4 B
2	Bank of America	USA	347.3 B
3	ICBC	China	270.0 B
4	China Merchants Bank	China	204.9 B
5	China Construction Bank	China	199.5 B
6	Wells Fargo & Co	USA	186.6 B
7	Agricultural Bank of China	China	169.7 B
8	Morgan Stanley	USA	154.4 B
9	Citigroup Inc	USA	148.7 B
10	Bank of China	China	138.9 B

Fig. 2.3 Market capitalization of global top 10 banks, own illustration based on ADV, 2021

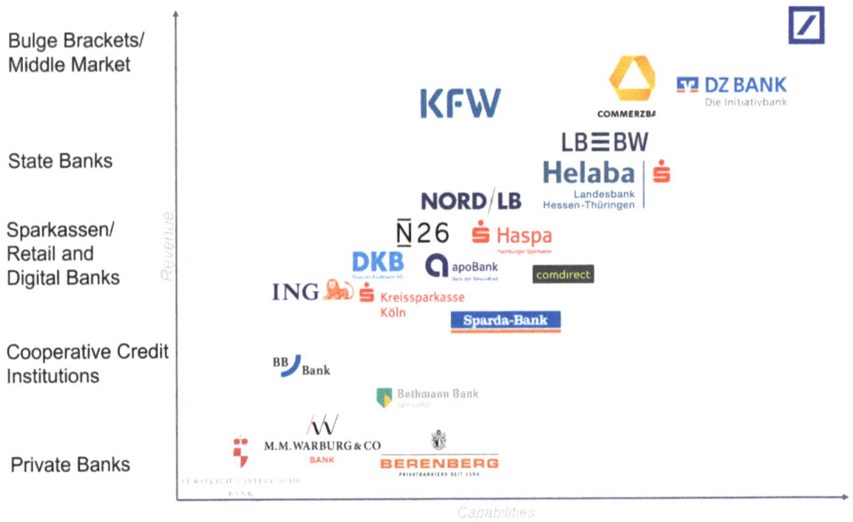

Fig. 2.4 German financial landscape, own illustration based on Banking Hub by ZEB, 2021

characterized by several different institutions. In addition to private banks such as Berenberg (which is one of the oldest private banks in the world), there are cooperative credit institutions that specialize in specific professions such as that of doctors or pharmacists. A significant portion of the market is occupied by the Sparkassen, such as Hamburger Sparkasse (Haspa) or Kreissparkasse Köln. German Sparkassen are specialized savings banks that enjoy a strong reputation in the local financial markets. These are in fact firms of high traditional value and constitute a large network of banks subject to an umbrella legislation that preserves the rights, obligations, and specialized status in the German market.

There is a lot of trust in these institutions because of their reputation for reliability. There are state banks that are responsible for the 16 states within Germany, such as Landesbank Baden-Württemberg. In spite of this, the banks with the most revenue are the middle-market banks and the bulge bracket banks. The only German bank that is considered a bulge bracket bank is Deutsche Bank, which is primarily due to its influence around the globe, its full service, and the volume of revenue that it generates.

Increasingly, there are new entrants to the global financial market who take advantage of the opportunity to disaggregate the elements of traditional banking in order to offer better services and targeted solutions to both business and retail clients. There have been many new players entering the financial industry over the years. Due to the advent of new technologies, fintechs have had the ability to unbundle the value chain of the banking sector (which focused on the overall satisfaction of the financial needs of clients) by focusing on a specific service or product (Ferrari, 2016).

A new environment has emerged where banks and other players are competing for the individual elements of the value chain. However, the parties are also forced to work closely together in nontraditional areas as well in order to jointly achieve their goals of profitability performance. It is for this reason that Fintech companies have started to offer their solutions and technology to banks as well. Meanwhile, banks have incorporated third-party services and products to cater to their value proposition to address the needs of their clients in a manner that is up to date with the modern and progressive developments in the global economy (De Lis & Ortún, 2018).

In the past few years, fintechs have started to transform the retail banking sector in a big way. A fintech company's ability to disrupt retail banking can be attributed to its innovative products and services, consumer-centric approach, and 24/7 access through social media and new nontraditional channels in order to disrupt retail banking (PwC, 2016).

In addition to fintechs, other technology conglomerates have also entered the financial sector to compete with incumbent banks. Several companies such as Apple, Alibaba, Amazon, Tencent, and Facebook have started to offer specific financial services and products around their digital ecosystems. By virtue of the millions of active users available to these companies, there is a possibility that the structure of the financial industry may be altered in the forthcoming years (De Lis & Ortún, 2018).

As these digital conglomerates have gained quick and large attention as well as acceptance, they also wield a certain level of influence within the financial market, and there are several characteristics that also empower them in their market position as new entrants amid a more traditional financial market. Taking the example of direct and indirect network effects, the company is able to generate a positive feedback loop that makes it possible for this company to become a market leader. One of the characteristics of these big companies is that their products and services generate a massive amount of data that can be used and exploited to improve their products and services. The result of this is that these companies have a significant competitive advantage over other players in the market (Bundeskartellamt & Autoritè de la concurrence, 2016).

Digitalization is one of the biggest challenges facing banks today. The banking industry has been focusing on products that would generate the most revenue for the bank ever since the 2008 financial crisis. In contrast, substantial strategic investments in technology and innovation were sacrificed to achieve the goal. Consequently, the banks have been unable to innovate customer journeys and experiences on time and remain as of date the biggest losers in a rapidly technologically advancing global market (Nayar, 2021).

If banks desire to continue existing in their home-turf, that is, in retail banking market over the next years, they may be forced to follow the lead or the pioneer role set by their digital competitors, such as the big tech companies. This forces traditional banks to imitate or learn from the offerings of the new entrants, while keeping the pressure of competitive behaviors high, encouraging them to offer higher quality services and more attractive customer journeys at comprehendible prices.

In the near future, it is predicted that channel diversification will become a key driver of financial sector growth (PwC, 2016). The banks are therefore required to focus on their customers' needs, and they must move toward providing a seamless and integrated banking experience for their clients in the future. Strategic alliances and cooperation with technology companies, consulting organizations, and research institutions are recommended to enhance the strategic and tactical positioning of incumbent banks in future.

References

BaFin. (2021a). *Alternative payment methods*. BaFin. https://www.bafin.de/EN/Aufsicht/FinTech/Bezahlverfahren/bezahlverfahren_node_en.html

BaFin. (2021b). *BaFin - Market entry. Bundesanstalt Für Finanzdienstleistungsaufsicht*. https://www.bafin.de/EN/Aufsicht/BankenFinanzdienstleister/Markteintritt/markteintritt_node_en.html

Bundesanstalt für Finanzdienstleistungsaufsicht. (2021). *Bankgeschäfte*. BaFin. https://www.bafin.de/DE/Aufsicht/BankenFinanzdienstleister/Markteintritt/Bankgeschaefte/bankgeschaefte_node.html;jsessionid=B70DCFAAFDFE69559EFD585F954C6F36.1_cid503

Bundeskartellamt, & Autoritè de la concurrence. (2016). *Competition law and data*. www.ec.europa.eu/competition/mergers/cases/decisions/m4731_20080311_20682_de.pdf,

Cambridge Dictionary. (2021). *BANK | Definition*. Cambridge Dictionary. https://dictionary.cambridge.org/de/worterbuch/englisch/bank.

CFI. (2020). *Bank corporate divisions - Explanation*. Corporate Finance Institute. https://corporatefinanceinstitute.com/resources/careers/jobs/bank-corporate-divisions/

Corporate Finance Institute. (2021a). *Bulge bracket investment banks - List of top global banks*. CFI.Com. https://corporatefinanceinstitute.com/resources/careers/companies/bulge-bracket-investment-banks-list/

Corporate Finance Institute. (2021b). *Middle market investment banks list - Investment overview*. CorporateFinanceInstitute. https://corporatefinanceinstitute.com/resources/careers/companies/middle-market-investment-banks/

De Lis, S. F., & Ortún, P. U. (2018). *Digital transformation and competition in the financial sector*. In BBVA Research. https://www.bbvaresearch.com/wp-content/uploads/2019/01/Digital-transformation-and-competition-in-the-financial-sector.pdf

European Central Bank. (2019). *Guide to assessments of licence applications – Licence applications in general*. Banking Supervision.

Ferrari, R. (2016). *FinTech impact on retail banking – From a universal banking model to banking verticalization*. The FinTech Book, pp. 248–252. doi:https://doi.org/10.1002/9781119218906.CH65.

Friesendorf, C., & Stern, J. (2020). Mangelnde Digitalisierung in der Finanzbranche. In *Digitalisierung des Auslandszahlungsverkehrs. essentials*. Springer. https://doi.org/10.1007/978-3-658-32738-5_1

Friesendorf, C., & Uedelhoven, L. (2021). Digital transformation of global mobility markets. In *Mobility in Germany. Springer briefs in business*. Springer. https://doi.org/10.1007/978-3-030-71849-7_1

Friesendorf, C., & Mir Haschemi, N. J. (2023). Private equity in Germany. In *Venture Capital for Digital Platform Start-ups. Springer business guides on the go*. Springer. https://doi.org/10.1007/978-3-031-33708-6

Kim, J. (2011). How modern banking originated: The London goldsmith-bankers' institutionalisation of trust. *Business History, 53*(6), 939–959. https://doi.org/10.1080/00076791.2011.578132

Labate, V. (2016). *Banking in the roman world - World history encyclopedia*. World History Encyclopedia. https://www.worldhistory.org/article/974/banking-in-the-roman-world/

Majaski, C. (2021). *Retail banking definition*. Investopedia. https://www.investopedia.com/terms/r/retailbanking.asp

Merkblatt zu den Geschäftsleitern gemäß KWG, ZAG und KAGB, 1 (2020) (testimony of BaFin).

N26. (2020). *What is a banking license? How does it protect customers? – N26*. N26. https://n26.com/en-eu/banking-license

Nayar, A. (2021). *Is it time for a retail banking revolution?* Forbes. https://www.forbes.com/sites/forbesfinancecouncil/2021/08/19/is-it-time-for-a-retail-banking-revolution/?sh=7eb53e7617d6

PwC. (2016). *Customers in the spotlight: How FinTech is reshaping banking*. PwC. https://www.pwc.com/gx/en/industries/financial-services/publications/fintech-is-reshaping-banking.html

Chapter 3
Decentralized Finance: Concept and Characteristics

3.1 Features of Decentralized Finance

One of the most famous papers written under the pseudonym Satoshi Nakamoto was published in the same year as that of the disastrous financial crisis, which was in the year 2008. This famous paper was titled Bitcoin: A Peer-to-Peer Electronic Cash System (Friesendorf & Uedelhoven, 2021; Friesendorf & Stern, 2020). For the very first time, a paper was formulated to generate a discussion on the idea of a new form of currency, namely the bitcoin. Therein, the concept of bitcoin, the overall plan, and the protocol that underlay the workings and intentions were laid out to the public. Bitcoin is ideally a form of decentralized finance (DeFi). As a DeFi product or instrument, it is aimed at creating a peer-to-peer version of e-money in which online financial transactions can be sent directly from one individual to another without the need to deal with a third party like a financial institution.

The vision is to create an independent form of currency that relies on pure transactional value and trust among peers. In simpler terms, this would be a peer-to-peer version of electronic money, or e-money (Nakamoto, 2008). Following the publication of this paper that drew a lot of attention from technology experts, bankers, government agencies, and media, there has been a growing continued interest in developing the vision of a decentralized financial system, thus marking a watershed for the growth and expansion of DeFi ideas and the DeFi market.

3.1.1 Decentralized Applications (dApps)

The purpose of DeFi is not to be a company or sell a single product; instead, it is to be a platform that encompasses a variety of products and services that can function as an alternative to traditional centralized institutions like insurance companies,

C. Friesendorf, A. Blütener, *Decentralized Finance (DeFi)*, Business Guides on the Go, https://doi.org/10.1007/978-3-031-37488-3_3

banks, money markets, or bonds. According to CoinGecko et al. (2020, p. 15), these services are provided under so-called Decentralized Applications (dApps), which are mainly deployed via the Ethereum ecosystem through the decentralized applications.

A decentralized application allows the user to consolidate all of their services under one roof, which opens up several possibilities for them in terms of what they can do with their services. Because of their composability, decentralized applications are sometimes referred to as money LEGOs (Tabora, 2021). There is, however, a requirement for smart contracts to lock in the assets needed to make dApps capable of processing transactions. In addition to this, smart contracts are also self-executing in nature. The transactions can therefore be executed without the need for the involvement of a third party, as we know from the traditional markets such as the intermediary role of a bank (Friesendorf & Mir Haschemi, 2023). We will go into greater detail about smart contracts in the next section.

3.1.2 *Total Value Locked*

Total Value Locked (TVL) refers to the total amount of assets or collaterals that are locked into DeFi dApps and is used as an indicator of the growth of the ecosystem within DeFi as a whole. A recent study has found that the total value locked up in DeFi dApps is currently 80.8 billion USD, compared with the TVL of only approximately 40 billion USD in March 2021 (Gackstatter, 2022). There is no doubt that the DeFi ecosystem has been growing rapidly in recent years as evidenced by this increase. Despite its rapid development and the growing interest in the DeFi ecosystem, it is important to keep in mind that at the moment, DeFi is still in an experimental and nascent phase and is still undergoing development. The development of many projects is still in their early stages, and they are being improved at a rapid rate. Compared to what it is today, DeFi may develop further and take a completely new form in the future. In addition to that, most of the components of DeFi have not yet been decentralized completely.

In this context, three categories can be used to measure the degree of decentralization in the DeFi dApps:

3.1.2.1 Centralized

A centralized dApp is characterized by the presence of centralized price feeds, custodial services, or interest rates that are constantly being determined by the central authority. There are a number of centralized DeFi dApps available on the market today, for example, Nexo, Celsius, Salt, or BlockFi.

3.1.2.2 Semi-Decentralized

There are a number of characteristics of semi-decentralized dApps, such as decentralized interest rate determination, decentralized price feed, and noncustodial dApps. For now, no permission is required for initiation of margin calls and decentralized development and updates on the platform. This offers freedom and flexibility of transactions and getting to know the ecosystem. The most prominent semi-decentralized decentralized apps are dYdX, Compound, bZx, and MakerDAO.

3.1.2.3 Fully Decentralized

Decentralization of an app is characterized by the fact that every component will be decentralized in a fully decentralized app. There are, however, no DeFi protocols that are entirely decentralized at this point in time, as they have not been developed yet. According to CoinGecko et al. (2020), the majority of DeFi dApps are currently at the stage of semi-decentralization. There is, however, a possibility that this may change in the future, as the DeFi ecosystem is striving to become a fully decentralized network.

DeFi is aimed at improving the financial landscape in general as part of its overall goal. In particular, it aims to improve the general accessibility of the system, the payment and clearance activity network, transparency, and centralization (CoinGecko et al., 2020).

3.1.3 Accessibility and Market Expansion

Having a savings account with a bank is a common practice in Europe and many other developed countries around the world. Despite this, there are many people around the world who do not have the same opportunity. The Global Findex Database is a tool of the World Bank that assesses financial development and obstacles hindering economic and financial growth. The database provides around 300 indicators on financial statistics that relate to ownership, payments, credit, savings, and financial resilience. The Global Findex Database of 2017 indicated that there are an estimated 1.7 billion unbanked people in the world.

Unbanked people are those adults who do not have access to basic savings accounts as a result of geographical obstacles, poverty, or a lack of trust in financial institutions, among many other factors. Despite the enormous growth in banking services in more than 3 billion of the population of the adult world, financial inclusion remains an unachieved target owing to a lack of education, gender gap, unemployment, natural disasters, and mostly poverty. As banking systems evolve into complex systems, it is becoming pertinent to offer financial literacy both in banked and unbanked populations to prevent an excess of debt and an income deterioration leading to poverty.

In Fig. 3.1, we present a heatmap of the unbanked adult population.

It is clear from the figure that nearly half of the unbanked people are located in seven economies around the world. China, Indonesia, India, Nigeria, Mexico, Bangladesh, and Pakistan are some of the countries on this list (World Bank & Global Findex, 2017). Women are the most unbanked group of people, which is also due to cultural differences between Eastern and Western cultures. Bringing technology to the unbanked, DeFi promises to make access to banking easier, especially for this target group. With the aid of technology and primary coaching in financial literacy and account handling, millions of people can be encouraged into the financial system. DeFi, as an instrument and an ecosystem, can empower several millions of people and thereby achieve market growth through financial inclusion.

Furthermore, the usage of DeFi is relatively simple as compared to the paperwork that is involved in the registration of a bank account, and its operation that may represent an expensive obstacle to populations in low-income levels. The DeFi dApp requires only an Internet connection and a mobile phone and does not require a waiting for long periods of time, for example, to verify one's identity, as required by traditional financial institutions across the world (CoinGecko et al., 2020). DeFi is truly a realistic option based on the statistics collected by international organizations such as the World Bank or the United Nations Development Program.

Estimates by the World Bank demonstrate that over two-thirds of the total number of unbanked adults in the world have access to the Internet and possess a smartphone. The DeFi platform could be more than a boon and a substantial gateway for these populations to acquire otherwise expensive or unreachable financial products and services. DeFi clearly aids greater participation and engagement in the economy and can have a strong impact on promoting the overall growth of financial and nonfinancial markets.

In addition, the DeFi movement aims to make finance more accessible, censorship-free, and borderless for everyone by progressively eliminating barriers. There are no discriminatory practices taking place in the ecosystem as DeFi protocols support the equality of playing fields for all (Schär, 2021). DeFi thereby holds great potential in enabling meritocratic and democratic practices, working, and culture in the financial world.

3.1.4 Remittance Convenience

There can be several obstacles that require overcoming when an individual, household, or company desires to transfer money from one bank account to another bank account in a foreign country. Such a remittance transaction is conditional upon several factors. Undertaking remittance transactions classically involve fees, compliance formalities, documentation, and a good amount of time and patience (Murphy, 2021). In this and because of this long-drawn process, a number of issues could

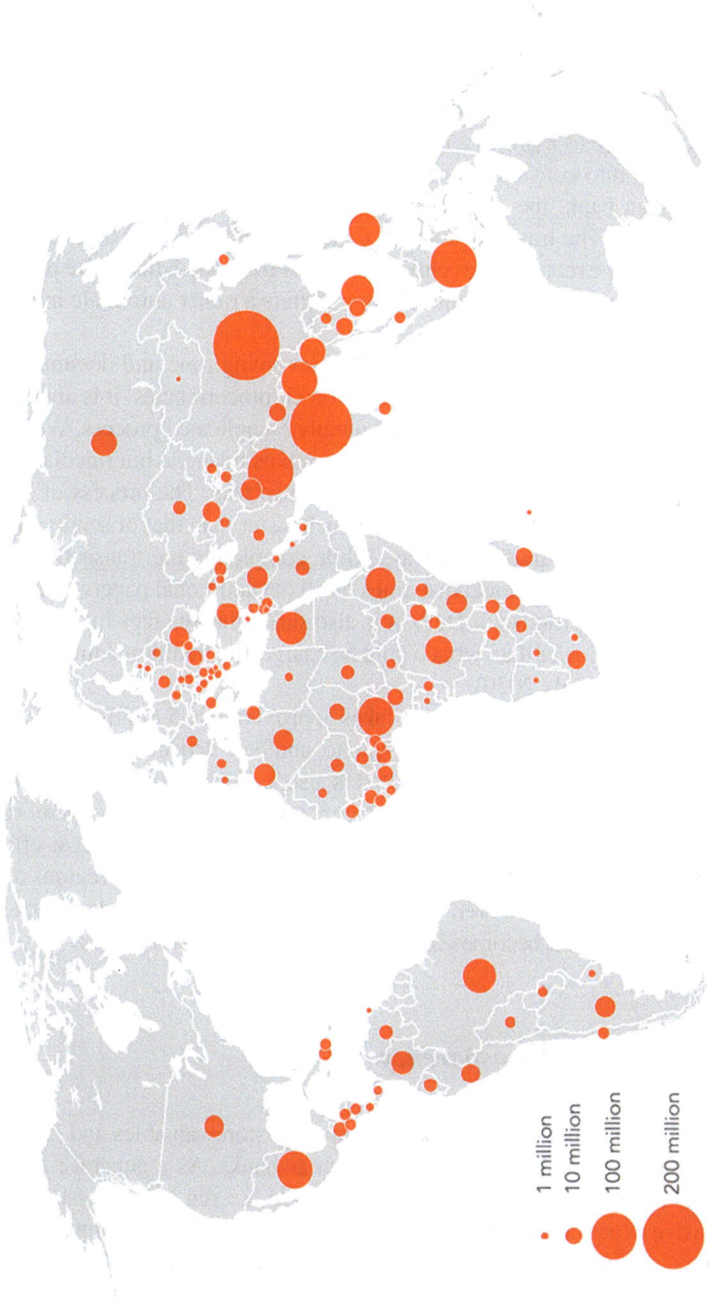

Fig. 3.1 Global heatmap of unbanked adults, own illustration based on Global Findex, 2017

arise regarding privacy concerns or legislation issues that could also be related to anti-money laundering.

In this process, one also establishes that there are also a string of fees or fee structures involved that need to be paid in order for remittances to pass through at every stage. This can make the process longer and more expensive. To illustrate, there are different fees that need to be paid when an individual living in Germany desires to send 500 € as a gift to a friend's bank account in the United States. A list of factors comes into consideration here, to note a few such as the exchange rate from the German bank, the international wire inbound-fee, and the international wire outbound-fee. The transfer process can take several working days depending on the location of the recipient (Boehlke, 2022). As illustrated, the entire process of transfer involves unpredictability and therefore offers a rather unreliable instrument of transaction.

Especially in such long-drawn transactions involving time and documentation, DeFi comes in handy. Because DeFi is based on cryptocurrencies, it is able to simplify what can otherwise be a lengthy and unduly complicated process. With DeFi, it is possible to bypass traditional incumbents such as financial intermediaries who take a substantial cut off the profits from remittance fees. The process of sending money between accounts with DeFi is also much faster than that of sending money between accounts in the traditional way. While completing the transaction, it will not be necessary to ask additional questions or fill out additional paperwork to facilitate it. As part of the promise of DeFi, it is also stated that the fees for transactions will be substantially lower than what would be charged by traditional financial institutions (CoinGecko et al., 2020).

In any part of the world right now, it takes approximately 5 min for a cryptocurrency to be transferred from one account to another, depending on the region (Hartmann, 2021). A small fee of 0.02 USD is also usually taken by these transfers, which is a lot less than what banks charge (up to 40 USD in some cases). Consequently, it can be said that DeFi is currently the fastest and most cost-effective option for transferring funds between accounts that are in different regions around the world. In the future, however, this is likely to change as DeFi becomes more visible and accepted as it becomes increasingly available to consumers.

3.1.5 Security via Transparency

It is without a doubt that one of the safest places to store valuables and funds is in regulated traditional financial institutions such as banks. As a general rule, traditional banks adhere to government regulations and are run by professionals who have extensive experience in the industry. In spite of this, these institutions are not without flaws. Even the largest and most prestigious banks can fail, as evidenced in the financial crisis of 2008. There are several examples of this, one of which is the case of Lehman Brothers or Washington Mutual. According to Lioudis (2021),

Lehman Brothers had assets worth 639 billion USD and Washington Mutual had deposits worth 188 billion USD (Lioudis, 2021).

It is still true, however, that both banks failed in the financial crisis that occurred in 2008 (Amadeo, 2021). As centralized players in the financial system, banks are also an important point of failure in the system since they play a central role in the entire political-economic system. Banks inherently absorb systemic risk that leads to an effect of contagion when even one interlinked bank fails. Lehman Brothers' collapse in 2008 was the catalyst for the financial contagion and eventually the series of financial crises that followed. With such enormous funds and power at their disposal, banks are a huge threat to the rest of the finance ecosystem if they fail.

Transparency is an additional crucial aspect of investing for regular investors that cannot be overlooked in the functioning of the savings and investment ecosystem. As a matter of fact, it is almost impossible for a regular investor to know what a bank does on a daily basis. Credit agencies, whose role is to rate the creditworthiness of companies, banks, and financial instruments, undertake the task of verification to aid qualitative decision-making on investments. There is much evidence in scientific and practitioner literature that credit agencies have not always delivered to the interests and goals of the investors. The credit agencies have previously rated high-risk mortgage-backed securities with a AAA rating (Ospina & Uhlig, 2018) in the past. Knowing this, it is safe to say that AAA ratings represent the safest and best investment option available to investors. When it came to the 2008 financial crisis, however, these ratings were falsely given by the rating agencies. Now this is a caveat that accompanies the practices of rating. Also here, the new option of DeFi would be a boon to those investors who value transparency and reliability of investment markets. With DeFi, both transparency and centralization have great potential for being improved.

To begin with, there is a public blockchain called Ethereum that forms the foundation for the DeFi protocols. There are a large number of blockchains such as Ethereum that can be described as open source and thereby accessible, mainly for the reason of transparency. The term open source refers to anything (in this case, a code) that is publicly accessible (RedHat, 2019) so that everyone can use the code to able to modify it and distribute it. As a result, all parties have access to information, which reduces the chances that any individual will i.e., can independently influence and, therefore, make a sub-optimal or bad decision without the knowledge of the others.

There are lines of code that make up the protocols on which DeFi runs. The protocols are unbreakable, and they do not allow cheating or exploitation of any kind. It is for this reason that DeFi works without discrimination. Code lines work exactly as they were programmed, and if there were any mistakes or flaws in the code, they would become obvious as soon as they were found. As a whole, the greatest strength of decentralized finance is that it is able to work without censorship and without the need for intermediaries, which is an important primary advantage of this system.

References

Amadeo, K. (2021). *Washington Mutual (WaMu): How it went bankrupt*. The Balance. https://www.thebalance.com/washington-mutual-how-wamu-went-bankrupt-3305620.

Boehlke, J. (2022). *How long does it take for a bill payment to go through online?* GoBankingRates.Com. https://www.gobankingrates.com/banking/checking-account/how-long-does-a-check-take-to-deposit/.

CoinGecko, L., Lau, D., Jin, T. S., Kho, K., Azmi, E., Lee, T., & Ong, B. (2020). *How to DeFi: Beginner* (1st ed.). Independently Published.

Friesendorf, C., & Stern, J. (2020). Mangelnde Digitalisierung in der Finanzbranche. In *Digitalisierung des Auslandszahlungsverkehrs. essentials*. Springer. https://doi.org/10.1007/978-3-658-32738-5_1

Friesendorf, C., & Uedelhoven, L. (2021). Digital transformation of global mobility markets. In *Mobility in Germany. Springer briefs in business*. Springer. https://doi.org/10.1007/978-3-030-71849-7_1

Friesendorf, C., & Mir Haschemi, N. J. (2023). Private equity in Germany. In *Venture Capital for Digital Platform Start-ups. Springer business guides on the go*. Springer. https://doi.org/10.1007/978-3-031-33708-6

Gackstatter, C. (2022). *2021: DeFi Pulse's Year in Indices*. DeFi Pulse. https://www.defipulse.com/blog/2021-defi-pulse-year-in-indices

Hartmann, T. (2021). *How long does it take to send Ethereum?* CaptainAltCoin.Com. https://captainaltcoin.com/how-long-does-it-take-to-send-ethereum/

Lioudis, N. (2021). *The collapse of Lehman brothers: A case study*. Investopedia. https://www.investopedia.com/articles/economics/09/lehman-brothers-collapse.asp

Murphy, C. B. (2021). *Remittance definition*. Investopedia. https://www.investopedia.com/terms/r/remittance.asp.

Nakamoto, S. (2008). *Bitcoin: A peer-to-peer electronic cash system*. Bitcoin.Org. www.bitcoin.org.

Ospina, J., & Uhlig, H. (2018). Mortgage-backed securities and the financial crisis of 2008: A post mortem. *SSRN Electronic Journal*. https://doi.org/10.2139/ssrn.3159552

RedHat. (2019). *What is open source?* RedHat.Com. https://www.redhat.com/en/topics/open-source/what-is-open-source

Schär, F. (2021). Decentralized finance: On blockchain- and smart contract-based financial markets. *Federal Reserve Bank of St. Louis Review, 103*(2), 153–174. https://doi.org/10.20955/R.103.153-74

Tabora, V. (2021). *Money Legos and composability as DeFi building blocks* | by Vincent Tabora | The Capital | Medium. The Capital. https://medium.com/the-capital/money-legos-and-composability-as-defi-building-blocks-efb1ad5e848e

World Bank, & Global Findex. (2017). *Findex 2017/The Unbanked*. In The Global Findex. https://globalfindex.worldbank.org/sites/globalfindex/files/chapters/2017 Findex full report_chapter2.pdf

Chapter 4
Decentralized Finance: Technical Basis

4.1 Blockchain as Centrifugal Technology

A blockchain is a digital ledger that is a record of multiple transactions that are shared, replicated, and distributed among a large network of nodes in order to keep track of each other (Friesendorf & Stern, 2020; Friesendorf & Uedelhoven, 2021). The blocks that make up the blockchain all store a different volume of transactions, and for every new transaction that is processed on the blockchain, a record of that transaction will be added to the ledger as it is recorded in the blockchain (Euromoney Learning, 2021).

The technology behind blockchain is widely recognized as being at the heart of many cryptocurrencies such as bitcoin or ether. In its original form, a blockchain was intended to be a distributed and open ledger that efficiently records the transaction between two parties in a way that makes it permanent and verifiable (Iansiti & Lakhani, 2017). This will make it harder for external parties to exploit, cheat, hack, or change the system in any way. The hacker would have to change every single block across all of the distributed ledgers if they were interested in altering one of the blocks in the chain as a result of tampering with the system. The effect of this would be that he would need to change every single block in the chain, which is bound to attract attention and thereby prevent system abuse or even financial crime.

4.1.1 Distributed Ledger Technology

In addition to this, the ledger in itself can also be programmed in such a way as to set off transactions automatically as they are entered. It is also important to note that a blockchain is not owned by a company. Due to the fact that the system is decentralized, it is in fact owned by everyone participating in this system. Distributed Ledger Technology (DLT) describes a decentralized system that is effectively

C. Friesendorf, A. Blütener, *Decentralized Finance (DeFi)*, Business Guides on the Go, https://doi.org/10.1007/978-3-031-37488-3_4

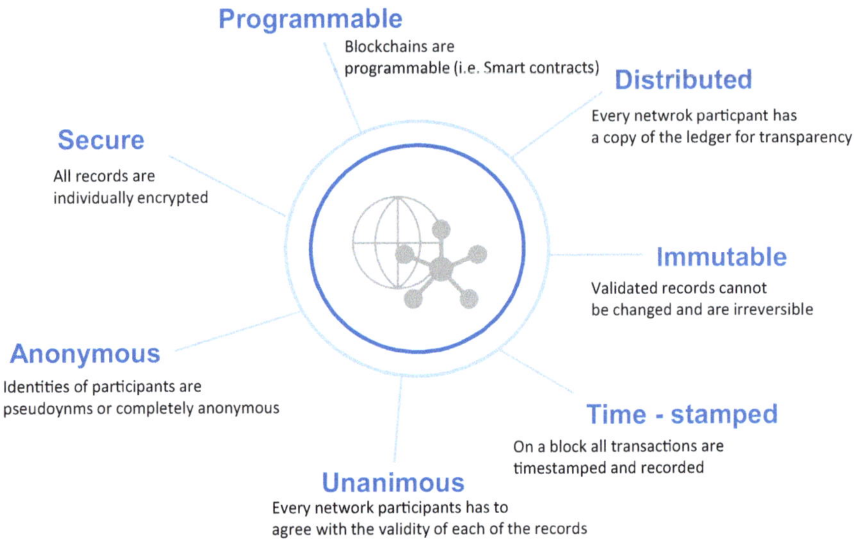

Fig. 4.1 Properties of DLT, own illustration based on Euromoney Learning (2021)

managed by multiple individuals within a network to ensure the security of the network. Blockchain technology is therefore a type of DLT, and its transactions are recorded using a signature called a hash, which is a type of cryptographic signature. Due to the fact that hashes are cryptographic and immutable, they increase the validity of the transactions that are recorded. In order to provide a better understanding of a DLT, the following figure shows its different properties. Figure 4.1 presents the properties of DLT.

DLTs, as mentioned above, are characterized by a variety of features among which programmability is a significant aspect. Also, the system is secure since all records are encrypted. Furthermore, it is anonymous since participants use pseudonyms or anonymous identities. DLT's validity is unanimous as every participant has previously agreed on its validity. DLT is immutable since it is based on hash signatures, which makes it impossible to reverse or change validated records. Transactions are also validated with a timestamp in each block of transactions. The final crucial aspect of the DLT is that it is a distributed and transparent system, with every participant of the network having a copy of the ledger (Euromoney Learning, 2021).

4.1.2 Non-fungible Tokes

Currently, Bitcoin and Ethereum are the two most prominent blockchains. Despite this, blockchain technology has more potential than just recording cryptocurrency transactions. Over the past few years, a new cryptographic asset called non-fungible tokens (NFTs) has been introduced on the blockchain. A unique set of metadata and identification codes is associated with NFTs. Due to this, they can be distinguished from one another. NFTs cannot be traded or exchanged for an equivalent asset, unlike other crypto assets such as bitcoin. In video games, for example, they can be used as art pieces and collectibles. The investment can, however, also be viewed as speculative in nature. It was reported that a piece of NFT known as "The Merge" made by a Korean artist called Pak was sold for USD 91.8 million in December 2021. However, most of the NFTs are unlikely to increase in value in the near future (Csiszar, 2022).

Since the technology is continuing to receive attention as a result of the volatility of cryptocurrencies and the hype created by the media, it is certain that the program will continue to expand as new blocks will be added and new network participants will appear to contribute to the system as it grows. It is anticipated that this continuous growth will ultimately increase the reliability and security of the technology in the long run.

According to Deloitte's survey on the global development of blockchain and cryptocurrencies conducted in 2021, these new technology-based financial contracting options could rapidly emerge as a strong alternative to traditional investment options in the future. According to Deloitte, 78% of the executives surveyed believe that digital assets will be a strong substitute or alternative to fiat currencies within five to ten years (Deloitte, 2021). Ultimately, it is predicted that every contract will be embedded into a code and be digitally stored as part of the blockchain's shared, transparent, and protected database in the future.

Whenever a payment is made, the system registers that a task has been completed, following which a process is checklisted as completed, and at the end of it an agreement is signed. In these series of actions, the blockchain is going to allow a digital signature as a finalization of the contract, which will be recorded and stored. This blockchain agreement or contract is thereby validated and identified within the blockchain. In the conduction of this system or scheme, there is little to no room for the involvement of intermediaries or third parties. Consequently, middlemen or intermediaries such as brokers, banks, and lawyers may become redundant as a result (Iansiti & Lakhani, 2017). Furthermore, the technology results in individuals, organizations, and machines freely interacting and transacting with one another. It is expected that once participants get used to the absence of intermediaries, there will be a steady devaluing of their role and need and may eventually result in an intermediary or bank-free financial system.

4.2 Ethereum's Robust Complementarity

Ethereum is an open-source platform for decentralized applications. It can be compared to a computer (that is accessible to the world) that cannot be shut down. The developers of this ecosystem are able to program smart contracts that are capable of controlling digital assets that are accessible to everyone worldwide.

4.2.1 Solidity and Ether

A 28-year-old Canadian-Russian programmer and co-founder of Bitcoin Magazine, Vitaly Dmitriyevich "Vitalik" Buterin proposed Ethereum in 2013 and later brought it to life. His vision for Ethereum is that it will serve as a "do it yourself" platform for decentralized applications that will one day decentralize the Internet. Any competent programmer who is proficient in Ethereum's programming language Solidity can create a decentralized program that cannot be controlled by anybody, not even the creator.

Due to the fact that Ethereum's blockchain is run by multiple independent computers around the world, the Ethereum ecosystem is completely decentralized. Once a program has been deployed, these independent computers (also referred to as nodes) ensure that the program operates as intended. Furthermore, Ethereum has its own currency, ETH (or Ether), which is used as a means of incentivizing the network. It is necessary for a programmer to pay with Gas in order to deploy their code. In computing terms, this refers to the amount of computational effort that is required to execute a smart contract or operation. Thus, programmers are motivated to write clean and effective code because a code that requires a higher level of computational effort is more expensive than one that requires less.

4.2.2 Gas Fee Pricing Model

A gas fee is entirely paid in ether, which was distributed in Ethereum's first initial coin offering, i.e., ICO (which funded the Ethereum platform) back in 2014 for 0.40 USD per ether. However, because of the increasing popularity of the network and cryptocurrencies, ETH is currently valued at 2755.20 EUR per ETH (CoinMarketCap, 2022). Just as Ether is a volatile currency, so is Gas, which fluctuates over time according to the network's demand. Since the network has a limited amount of computational capacity, the Gas price increases as more people interact with the network, deploy programs, and trade ETH. Conversely, if there is less traffic in the network, then the price of Gas decreases (CoinGecko et al., 2020).

The following example describes how Gas prices are calculated in the Ethereum network:

Gas Prices Are Usually Expressed in gwei.
Gas prices are calculated using the assumption that 1 gwei equals 0.000000001 ether (the cryptocurrency Ethereum).

Assuming that the execution of a smart contract, for example, to transfer tokens, requires 21.000 gas units, then the average market price of gas is 3 gwei. This can be calculated as follows:

21.000 gas times 3 gwei equals 63.000 gwei, which is equivalent to 0.000063 Ethereum. To validate and process this transaction, a user must pay a gas fee of 0.000063 ETH to the network (CoinGecko et al., 2020).

It is also possible to set gas fees manually. The first transactions to go through when the network encounters a bottleneck due to a high volume of transactions are those with the highest gas fees, followed by those with lower gas fees. In addition, the system queues transactions with a gas fee that is too low. Therefore, it can be said that cheaper transactions that have a lower than the average gas fee take longer to be finalized and added to the Ethereum blockchain than the more expensive ones.

4.2.3 Decentralized Autonomous Organization

Ethereum is capable of issuing cryptocurrency and developing decentralized applications (dApps) as well as building Decentralized Autonomous Organizations (DAOs). In short, a DAO is a completely autonomous organization that is not governed by a company or a single individual (CoinGecko et al., 2020). Instead, DAOs are controlled by code that is based on smart contracts, which enable them to replace or substitute traditional organizations. Due to the fact that DAOs are based on code, they operate transparently, are protected from outside human intervention, and cannot be influenced by outside influences. As opposed to traditional organizations, a decision would be made only by token voting and not by a board of members (Shuttleworth, 2021).

Ethereum offers several advantages and possibilities. Decentralization of the network depends primarily on the technology of smart contracts. We will discuss smart contracts in detail in the next section.

4.3 Smart Contract Efficiency

Smart contracts are similar to traditional contracts, except that they are digital. It is important to note that a smart contract is a programmed contract that is stored in a blockchain. In 1997, a computer scientist and law scholar named Nick Szabo developed the term "smart contract" to describe a distributed ledger on which contracts could be stored (Vigliotti, 2021).

Self-executing smart contracts allow counterparties to set specific terms of a trade without the assistance of a third party such as a lawyer or a bank. Figure 4.2 illustrates in detail the process of a smart contract and compares it with the current process of a contractual agreement.

Figure 4.2 illustrates Alice's desire to purchase a home from Bob. Consequently, she relies on intermediaries such as insurance companies, brokers, and lawyers to set up contracts between her and Bob. These intermediaries, of course, charge a fee for their services. With a smart contract, Alice is able to program the contract herself.

For example, she might:

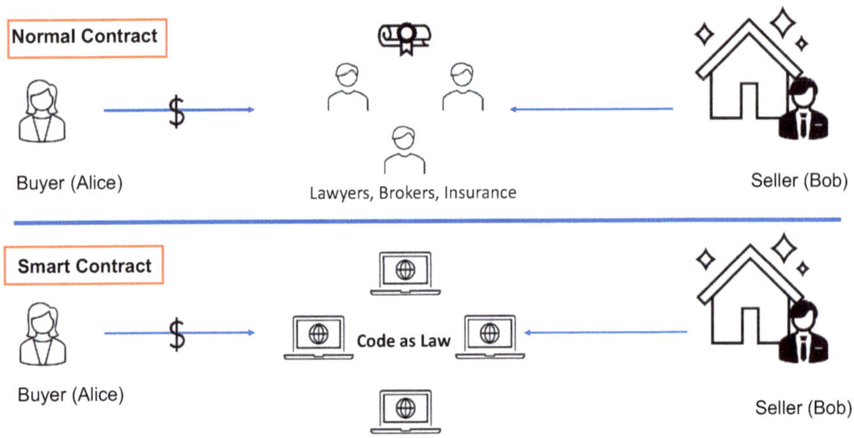

Fig. 4.2 Smart versus normal contracts, own illustration based on CB Insights, 2021

1. Ensure that the current date is correct.
2. Is able to reach an agreement with Bob that he must paint the walls before February 1.
3. Sends Bob 5000 Ethereum on February 1 for this property.
4. Takes possession of the house on March 1.

A smart contract allows Alice and Bob to avoid costly intermediaries and make the transaction transparent for all parties involved. In addition, both Bob and Alice receive a greater return on their investment. In this case, Bob can keep a larger portion of the profit for himself, while Alice does not have to pay more than the house's worth since neither party has to pay large fees to intermediaries. The only cost they would have with a smart contract is the gas fee for deploying the smart contract in the blockchain.

Smart contracts are coded according to a simple "if, then" logic. Therefore, if a requirement is met, the smart contract will execute the transaction as specified. It is possible to combine several smart contracts in order to fulfill more complex transactions and processes. This operation is known as a decentralized application (dApp), as discussed in the previous sections.

Blockchain technology makes smart contracts trustworthy (Friesendorf & Mir Haschemir, 2023). As a result, they inherit some of the properties associated with DLTs. Just like a distributed ledger technology, a smart contract is distributed and immutable. Once a smart contract has been created, it cannot be modified again. The code cannot be tampered with by any third party. Consequently, if Bob, the seller of the house, wanted to change the code in order to obtain more money from Alice, it would be impossible to change the code and defraud her.

A distributed smart contract also means that every participant in the network validates the outcome of the contract. It is therefore probable that if Bob were to force the contract to release the 5000 ETH from Alice before he has painted the walls, the other people on the network would notice his attempt to deceive Alice and invalidate it. The use of smart contracts provides a safe and competitive alternative to traditional contracts since it is virtually impossible to interfere with them.

References

CoinGecko, L., Lau, D., Jin, T. S., Kho, K., Azmi, E., Lee, T., & Ong, B. (2020). *How to DeFi: Beginner* (1st ed.). Independently Published.

CoinMarketCap. (2022). *Ethereum (ETH) Kurs, Grafiken, Marktkapitalisierung | CoinMarketCap*. CoinMarketCap. https://coinmarketcap.com/de/currencies/ethereum/

Csiszar, J. (2022). *How to get rich by investing in NFTs*. GOBankingRates. https://www.gobankingrates.com/investing/crypto/how-to-get-rich-investing-nfts/

Deloitte. (2021). Deloitte's 2021 global blockchain survey. *Deloitte Insights*. https://www2.deloitte.com/content/dam/insights/articles/US144337_Blockchain-survey/DI_Blockchain-survey.pdf

Euromoney Learning. (2021). *Blockchain explained: What is blockchain?*. Euromoney.Com. https://www.euromoney.com/learning/blockchain-explained/what-is-blockchain

Friesendorf, C., & Stern, J. (2020). Mangelnde Digitalisierung in der Finanzbranche. In *Digitalisierung des Auslandszahlungsverkehrs. essentials*. Springer. https://doi.org/10.1007/978-3-658-32738-5_1

Friesendorf, C., & Uedelhoven, L. (2021). Digital transformation of global mobility markets. In *Mobility in Germany. Springer briefs in business*. Springer. https://doi.org/10.1007/978-3-030-71849-7_1

Friesendorf, C., & Mir Haschemi, N. J. (2023). Private equity in Germany. In *Venture Capital for Digital Platform Start-ups. Springer business guides on the go*. Springer. https://doi.org/10.1007/978-3-031-33708-6

Iansiti, M., & Lakhani, K. R. (2017). The truth about blockchain. *Harvard Business Review*. https://hbr.org/2017/01/the-truth-about-blockchain#

Shuttleworth, D. (2021). *What is a DAO and how do they work?*. ConsenSys. https://consensys.net/blog/blockchain-explained/what-is-a-dao-and-how-do-they-work/

Vigliotti, M. G. (2021). What do we mean by smart contracts? Open challenges in smart contracts. *Frontiers in Blockchain, 0*, 45. https://doi.org/10.3389/FBLOC.2020.553671

Chapter 5
Decentralized Finance: Categories

5.1 Decentralized Stablecoins

Functional digital economy are complete only with the transition of real-world financial and currency products into digital variants (Friesendorf & Stern, 2020). Such digital products then serve as engines or drivers of growth into incumbent and new markets such as experienced in retail, infrastructure, and mobility segments (Friesendorf & Uedelhoven, 2021). The digital economy through its offer of innovation-based transformation on the overall offers incentives for new entrants such as start-up entrepreneurship (Friesendorf & Mir Haschemir, 2023). In this regard, a key component of new currency systems is the centrality of decentralized stablecoins. A decentralized stablecoin is a cryptocurrency class that is backed by reserve assets in order to maintain price stability. Cryptocurrency prices are usually highly volatile, with intraday swings exceeding 10%. As a result, cryptocurrencies are considered speculative and high-risk investments. Stablecoins, on the other hand, aim to mitigate the risks and volatility associated with cryptocurrencies by pegging their value to an alternative stable asset such as the euro or the dollar (Hayes, 2022).

We will discuss decentralized stablecoins in detail in the following chapters, as they are one of the key use cases for the DeFi movement.

5.2 Decentralized Derivatives

A derivative is a contract whose value is derived from an underlying asset, such as a stock, index, currency, interest rate, or commodity (Fernando, 2022). In such a contract, the price is determined by the fluctuations of the underlying assets. This financial contract is usually concluded between two or more parties who are able to

C. Friesendorf, A. Blütener, *Decentralized Finance (DeFi)*, Business Guides on the Go, https://doi.org/10.1007/978-3-031-37488-3_5

trade over the counter or on an exchange based on the assets involved. As their prices are based on fluctuations, they are generally leveraged instruments with an increased risk, but also an increased potential reward (Birken & Schmidt, 2021). As a result, the trader is able to use a derivative in order to hedge his position in order to decrease the risks associated with a particular transaction.

5.2.1 *Future*

A trader can choose from a variety of derivatives, such as a future. A saddle manufacturer might be interested in hedging himself against any unexpected increases in leather prices. For this reason, he can purchase a futures contract from his supplier to deliver a specific amount of leather at a particular date of delivery in the future at a price agreed upon in the past.

5.2.2 *Forwards*

In addition, there is also a type of derivative known as a forward contract. Futures contracts are similar to these types of contracts. Generally, they are private contracts between two players and traded over the over-the-counter market. Due to the fact that forwards are instruments that operate on unregulated markets, they carry a greater risk of default, which makes them a less preferred investment instrument for the average investor (Birken & Schmidt, 2021).

5.2.3 *Options*

Derivatives can also take the form of options. Options differ from forwards and futures in that they are nonbinding. Options are agreements between two parties to purchase at a particular time for a certain price. It should be noted, however, that the party who is buying is not obligated to act on it. Option contracts are nonbinding and generally require the buyer to purchase a premium that represents a portion of the value agreed to. As with futures, options can be traded on exchanges and over the counter (Birken & Schmidt, 2021).

5.2.4 *Swaps*

As a final type of derivative, swaps are contracts between two parties to exchange liabilities or cash flows in order to generate profits or reduce costs. In general, these contracts are based on currencies, credit defaults, commodities, and interest rates.

Swaps are typically available only over the counter and have a high counterparty risk. Furthermore, they are normally only available to companies and financial institutions and are not intended for individuals (Birken & Schmidt, 2021).

Commonly, these types of contracts are traded on centralized platforms such as traditional banks. DeFi has, however, recently begun to establish decentralized derivative markets that connect buyers and sellers directly.

Similar to other DeFi categories, DeFi derivative services are backed by collateral pools. Furthermore, users of the network are permitted to trade synthetic exposures without having to hold them themselves. As decentralized derivatives constitute a significant use case for the DeFi movement, they will be further discussed in the next chapters.

5.3 Decentralized Payments

The decentralized and trustless transfer of assets between two parties is one of the key functions of cryptocurrency. With the rapid growth of DeFi, more and more innovative and creative payment methods are being introduced and experimented with. Instead of providing payments in the form of transactions, decentralized payments aim to provide payments in the form of streams. In this way, more potential applications of assets or money can be realized in the near future.

5.4 Decentralized Lending and Borrowing

In a centralized financial system, a bank account is required to utilize financial services. Nearly 1.7 billion unbanked individuals lack access to a bank account. Additionally, a person or a company must meet certain requirements in order to borrow money from a traditional financial institution. These restrictions include:

Pertinent Restrictions

- Creditworthiness
- Necessary to provide adequate collateral
- The provision of a personal guarantee
- Experience in the business world
- Invoices and financial statements

It is also necessary for the borrower to demonstrate to the bank that he or she is capable of repaying the loan and is deserving of it.

Consequently, decentralized lending and borrowing could remove the barrier for the unbanked and enable anyone to obtain a loan by collateralizing their digital assets. Additionally, users can also earn a yield on their financial assets, which opens up the possibility of participating in the lending market by contributing their digital assets to lending pools in order to earn interest on them. Anyone can take advantage of decentralized lending and borrowing without the need for a bank account. As decentralized lending and borrowing is a major use case for the DeFi movement, we discuss this in detail in the next chapters.

5.5 Decentralized Exchange

Users utilize exchanges to trade cryptocurrencies with other parties. Binance and Coinbase are two of the most prominent exchanges. Since these exchanges are centralized, they act as custodians and intermediaries of the cryptocurrencies or assets that are traded. Therefore, users of centralized exchanges such as Binance and Coinbase do not have complete control over their assets. Therefore, users are putting their own assets at risk if an exchange is hacked, which would result in them being unable to repay their debts.

A decentralized exchange aims to reduce the risk for users and to resolve the issue of giving up control of their digital assets. Due to the fact that users will not be required to store their assets on centralized exchanges, they will not be required to trust these exchanges in order to remain solvent. As decentralized exchanges are a central use case of the DeFi movement, they will be further discussed in the next chapters.

5.6 Decentralized Wealth Management

Traditionally, investors rely on wealth managers to allocate and manage their investment portfolios. In general, these services are provided to wealthy individuals as well as ultra-high net worth individuals (UHNWI) and families, as explained in Chaps. 2 and 3. A fund manager usually assembles a financial product that is regulated, such as an exchange-traded fund, mutual fund, private equity interest, or separately managed account. Wealth managers package products for asset allocations, which are then distributed to clients through brokers and financial advisors (Gogel et al., 2021). In general, these services come with relatively high service fees such as hourly fees, per-plan fees, flat fees, and other financial advisor fees.

It is also possible for individuals to manage their cash flow and oversee their assets in order to generate a return on their investment. There are two types of wealth management—passive and active. The type of wealth management described above is active wealth management. On the other hand, passive wealth management does not require a management team to oversee and manage the portfolio. An attempt is made to replicate as closely as possible the performance of a specific benchmark.

In decentralized finance, some protocols have already begun to mimic passive fund management, which is conducted in a decentralized manner. As a result of DeFi's transparency, the user is able to track his funds, see how they are being managed, and determine the costs associated with the services. We will elaborate further on wealth management in the next chapter since it is a vital use case for the DeFi movement.

5.7 Decentralized Lotteries

In the coming years, DeFi is expected to continue to grow, resulting in more disruptive and creative financial applications that are expected to remove intermediaries and democratize access to finance. There is a possibility that DeFi could revolutionize the lottery industry. In the case of a lottery, there is a custodian who is responsible for the pooled capital. By locking pooled assets into smart contracts on blockchains such as Ethereum, DeFi could eliminate the need for custodianship by eliminating the need for custodianship.

A simple lottery dApp can be linked to a DeFi dApp with DeFi's modularity, creating another decentralized application that can be developed with DeFi's modularity. PoolTogether is one of the most popular DeFi dApps that can be used to conduct decentralized lotteries. Those who participate in this decentralized lottery will have the opportunity to pool their capital, which will then be invested into the DeFi lending dApps. The winner of the lottery receives interest from the pooled capital of all lottery participants at the end of the game. As opposed to centralized lotteries, decentralized lotteries return all capital invested in buying lottery tickets to the participants.

5.8 Decentralized Insurance

The concept of insurance is an essential part of the life of a modern European citizen on a day-to-day basis. There is generally a consensus, especially in the traditional financial industry, that insurance is a centralized means of managing risk that offers individuals a measure of financial protection against unfortunate incidents in the event of an unforeseen event. Another way of putting it is that an insurance provides some compensation in anticipation of events of loss in order to minimize that loss. In most cases, individuals purchase insurance for a variety of reasons, including their homes, cars, pets, lives, and health.

In the DeFi world, there is also a potential use case for a decentralized insurance service. Considering the potential payout that can be generated from a token locked in a smart contract, each token that is locked in a smart contract is vulnerable to exploits. While most network protocols are audited on a regular basis, there is no way of knowing if smart contracts are truly 100% secure as there is always the risk of hacking that could lead to the loss of digital assets (Blockchain Simplified, 2021). In particular, when dealing with vast amounts of digital assets, it would be beneficial to highlight the possibility of the need for insurance. There will be a discussion of the DeFi use case for decentralized insurance in the following chapters.

References

Birken, E. G., & Schmidt, J. (2021). *What are derivatives? – Forbes advisor*. Forbes Advisor. https://www.forbes.com/advisor/investing/derivatives/

Blockchain Simplified. (2021). *Decentralized Insurance – An emerging sector in DeFi. Medium*. https://medium.com/@blockchain_simplified/decentralized-insurance-an-emerging-sector-in-defi-79bd84502cab.

Fernando, J. (2022). *Derivative definition*. Investopedia. https://www.investopedia.com/terms/d/derivative.asp#.

Friesendorf, C., & Stern, J. (2020). Mangelnde Digitalisierung in der Finanzbranche. In *Digitalisierung des Auslandszahlungsverkehrs. essentials*. Springer. https://doi.org/10.1007/978-3-658-32738-5_1

Friesendorf, C., & Uedelhoven, L. (2021). Digital transformation of global mobility markets. In *Mobility in Germany. Springer briefs in business*. Springer. https://doi.org/10.1007/978-3-030-71849-7_1

Friesendorf, C., & Mir Haschemi, N. J. (2023). Private equity in Germany. In *Venture Capital for Digital Platform Start-ups. Springer business guides on the go*. Springer. https://doi.org/10.1007/978-3-031-33708-6

Gogel, D., Baker-Taylor, T., Cloots, A. S., Forster, B., Lazaro, J., Schär, F., & Sokolin, L. (2021). *DeFi beyond the hype*. The Wharton School. https://wifpr.wharton.upenn.edu/wp-content/uploads/2021/05/DeFi-Beyond-the-Hype.pdf

Hayes, A. (2022). *Stablecoin definition*. Investopedia. https://www.investopedia.com/terms/s/stablecoin.asp

Chapter 6
Decentralized Finance: Safety and Security

6.1 Financial Risks

As stated, cryptocurrencies are prone to volatility, with intraday swings of over 10% being common. Because of the unpredictable nature of the cryptocurrency market, there is a higher risk when investing in digital assets as significant price drops are not unusual and are common in the market for digital assets (Friesendorf & Stern, 2020; Friesendorf & Mir Haschemi, 2023). Moreover, if all participants in a network were to withdraw their money at the same time from the liquidity pool in the network, then the liquidity pool would run out (called a "bank run").

As it is with every environment, there are also malicious developers in the DeFi movement as well. As a result of these developers having programmed in the so-called back doors into their protocols, they are able to pull tokens from smart contracts and therefore steal from their users through these back doors. As a result, this method of pulling rugs is called a "rug-pulling scheme" (Verbiest, 2022).

There is also a possibility that so-called flash loans can be used as a tool to extort borrowers from DeFi loans. In most cases, these loans do not require collateral and usually involve smaller amounts of money as well. It is unique in the sense that the borrower must pay back the debt at the same time as they borrow it. If the agreement cannot be renegotiated, the lender will be able to revoke it. There is a possibility that a malicious actor from outside could manipulate the market in this case through flash loans. Furthermore, flash loans can also be used for the exploitation of lending protocols to gain a personal advantage (Weston, 2021).

C. Friesendorf, A. Blütener, *Decentralized Finance (DeFi)*, Business Guides on the Go, https://doi.org/10.1007/978-3-031-37488-3_6

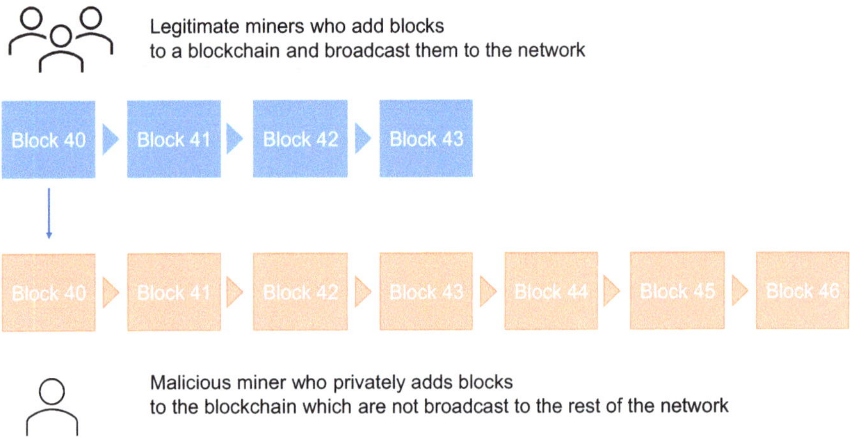

Fig. 6.1 Attack on blockchain, own illustration based on SEBA Bank, 2020

6.2 Technology Risks

There are several technological risks associated with DeFi that may have an adverse effect on the user or even the platform as a whole. In most cases, these risks occur as a result of issues with software, protocol, or hardware. Due to the fact that DeFi relies on blockchain technology, there is an increased risk that the system is vulnerable to a blockchain attack called a 51% attack, as demonstrated in Fig. 6.1.

Typically, a group or individual has control of over 50% of the network hash rate on a blockchain, which means that they can influence the changes that are made to various blocks that store transactions. For example, if a malicious person wanted to double spend digital assets, they would transform Block 40's transaction (Bitcoins being traded for ETH at an exchange) into an entirely different type of digital asset. As they transform the block, they mine more blocks where they will later be able to have a more extensive chain by the time they finish. They are sending the ETH they have transformed to themselves in their own private block, rather than sending it to the exchange or to anyone else. As a result, they are gaining ETH and Token A in this transaction. Because the malicious miner's chain is longer than the network's chain, the network accepts the longer chain of the miner due to the rule of the longest chain (the chain with the most work done by it). This means that previous transactions are going to be erased, as a result of which the malicious miner will be able to double spend his tokens several times (SEBA Bank, 2020).

Furthermore, there are also other risks for the blockchain, such as network congestion or bugs that can make it more difficult and more costly for the blockchain to function, in addition to attacks (Friesendorf & Uedelhoven, 2021; Weston, 2022). Cyberattacks are not only targeting blockchains, but also protocols when it comes to cyberattacks. There are also some bugs that are protocol-specific that could be exploited by some users.

6.3 Procedural Risks

When dealing with DeFi, it is also necessary to take into account the procedural risks that are involved. The majority of these concerns are related to security risks that may be encountered by users when using DeFi services and products. In this case, phishing through emails could be one of the possible attacks. A malicious person could gain access to the users' data if they sent an email to them mirroring the data of a particular DeFi product or service, or they could transfer malicious code to the user's computer through which malicious browser add-ons or software will be installed to gain control of the data or assets of the user. Another possible attack is the duplication of the service or website itself in order to lure customers to the website in order to gain sensitive personal information from them (see Iredale, 2020).

6.4 Regulatory Risks

The DeFi network has a global reach that enables peer-to-peer transactions anywhere in the world without having to deal with intermediaries. It is also important to note that these transactions are also anonymous. Regulators are trying to mitigate the risks associated with this kind of activity, as a means to limit these violations. Consumer protection, terrorist financing, and money laundering are some of the most prominent regulatory risks (Verbiest, 2022). The regulatory environment of DeFi will be explained in greater detail in the following chapters.

To conclude, it is important to note that developers are working tirelessly in order to address and improve the vulnerabilities within the DeFi system. The government is also in the process of introducing new action plans and mechanisms on how to effectively manage these risks. In spite of this, the process of implementing DeFi is still ongoing and the ecosystem continues to grow (Friesendorf & Stern, 2020).

In addition to the media attention and hype that DeFi has been receiving as more and more mainstream users discover the networks, there is a further problem that is arising. To invest on these platforms, only mature and sophisticated investors have been investing actively on account of the DeFi market being highly speculative and highly volatile. By including mainstream users in the equation, the need for risk management and regulatory considerations increases (Werbach, 2021).

Despite its phenomenal growth, this technology is still maturing and has not yet reached its full potential despite its enormous growth. There will still be a need for users to work carefully and responsibly with the environment since regulatory measures and safety protocols have yet to be fully developed.

References

Friesendorf, C., & Stern, J. (2020). Mangelnde Digitalisierung in der Finanzbranche. In *Digitalisierung des Auslandszahlungsverkehrs. essentials*. Springer. https://doi.org/10.1007/978-3-658-32738-5_1

Friesendorf, C., & Uedelhoven, L. (2021). Digital transformation of global mobility markets. In *Mobility in Germany. Springer briefs in business*. Springer. https://doi.org/10.1007/978-3-030-71849-7_1

Friesendorf, C., & Mir Haschemi, N. J. (2023). Private equity in Germany. In *Venture Capital for Digital Platform Start-ups. Springer business guides on the go*. Springer. https://doi.org/10.1007/978-3-031-33708-6

Iredale, G. (2020). *A guide to risks in DeFi and how to manage them. 101 Blockchains*. https://101blockchains.com/risks-in-defi/

SEBA Bank. (2020). *Are blockchains that safe? The Bridge*. https://theblockchaintest.com/uploads/resources/SEBA - Research the Bridge are Blockchains that Safe - 2020 - Sep.pdf

Verbiest, T. (2022, January 22). *How should DeFi be regulated? A European approach to decentralization*. Cointelegraph. https://cointelegraph.com/news/how-should-defi-be-regulated-a-european-approach-to-decentralization

Werbach, K. (2021). *The opportunities and dangers of decentralizing finance - Knowledge@Wharton*. Knowledge @ Wharton. https://knowledge.wharton.upenn.edu/article/opportunities-dangers-decentralizing-finance/

Weston, G. (2021). *3 major DeFi lending risks that you should know. 101 Blockchains*. https://101blockchains.com/defi-lending-risks/

Weston, G. (2022). *Uniswap vs SushiSwap - Key differences. 101 Blockchains*. https://101blockchains.com/uniswap-vs-sushiswap/

Chapter 7
Decentralized Finance: Regulation

7.1 Financial Action Task Force (FATF)

Regulation secures the functionality of the economic system of which the financial and the digital economies are central aspects (Friesendorf & Uedelhoven, 2021; Friesendorf & Stern, 2020). The introduction of new venues and products in capital financing required necessary yet unimpinging regulation that does not stifle new entrants such as start-ups in the field (Friesendorf & Mir Haschemi, 2023). Digital assets and digital economy continue to be radically new innovation that needs careful introduction and eventual integration in the real-world economy. As of October 28, 2021, an update regarding guidance on digital assets was issued by the international organization FATF (Financial Action Task Force) as a part of their financial action task force. By evaluating whether decentralized finance (DeFi) projects should be ruled under the VASP (Virtual Asset Service Provider) regime, the FATF is seeking to define regulations on how to identify responsible actors within the DeFi network by defining whether projects should be ruled under the VASP (Virtual Asset Service Provider) regime. A number of obligations are imposed under the VASP regime, such as Counter Terrorist Financing (CFT), Anti Money Laundering (AML), and others.

Here below is a visual overview of the six pillars of the FATF's work. Figure 7.1 provides a framework of preventive ideals.

In order to test DeFi products, the FATF raises the following questions that follow the process of due diligence to ensure compliance with rules and regulations:

C. Friesendorf, A. Blütener, *Decentralized Finance (DeFi)*, Business Guides on the Go, https://doi.org/10.1007/978-3-031-37488-3_7

Fig. 7.1 Financial Action Task Force (FATF), own illustration

FATF Due Diligence

Is there any control over the assets or the protocol itself by a person or entity?

Is there a commercial relationship between a person or entity and its customer, even if the relationship is exercised via a smart contract?

Can a person or entity profit from the provision of a service to a customer?

Are there any other indicators that an owner/operator is involved?

There is a requirement for operators and developers to carry out this test before they launch their product or service to the public. They will also need to take steps in order to mitigate and manage risk continuously once the product or service is launched. The FATF requires that the state or government be involved in a DeFi project that is already regulated by VASP if there is no operator or owner. According to FATF guidelines, a DeFi project is not subject to VASP if it is fully decentralized according to the guidance of the FATF (Fanusie, 2021).

7.2 Markets in Crypto Assets

It is not only the FATF that has been proposing guidance on the regulation of DeFi, but the European Union has also developed a regulatory framework for the regulation of digital assets. On November 24, 2021, the European Council submitted the MiCA (Markets in Crypto Assets) framework to the European Parliament for its consideration, with the expectation that it would be adopted by the end of 2022. In order to implement the framework, a centralized approach has been adopted. In this document, there is guidance on how you can identify the provider who is responsible for offering the products or services. In contrast, this does not work for decentralized stablecoins or decentralized exchanges.

Regulators should also consider enacting a regulatory system that takes into account the decentralized and automated nature of these systems in order to create a regulatory system that is both effective and efficient. There is also a need for investors to be aware of the potential risks posed by an unregulated system in terms of financial, compliance, and technological issues that could arise.

7.3 Environment, Social, and Governance (ESG)

Apart from the MiCA framework, the European Union is also imposing new regulations in the area of environmental, social, and governance (ESG). Figure 7.2 provides an overview of the general ESG categories and aspects that require to be considered in regulatory design that addresses DeFi.

It is evident from Fig. 7.2 that there are three prominent key components that must be followed in order for ESG investing to be successful (Friesendorf, 2022). To qualify for the environmental criteria, a company must show how it interacts with the environment. This can be in the form of how much the company manages its natural resources, how much energy the company consumes, or how the company treats its animals. In the second criterion, social, the company's relationships with its customers and other stakeholders are measured. It could be a good idea to ask the company how they treat their employees, if they donate a certain amount of their profits to a good cause, or if they encourage their employees to volunteer for

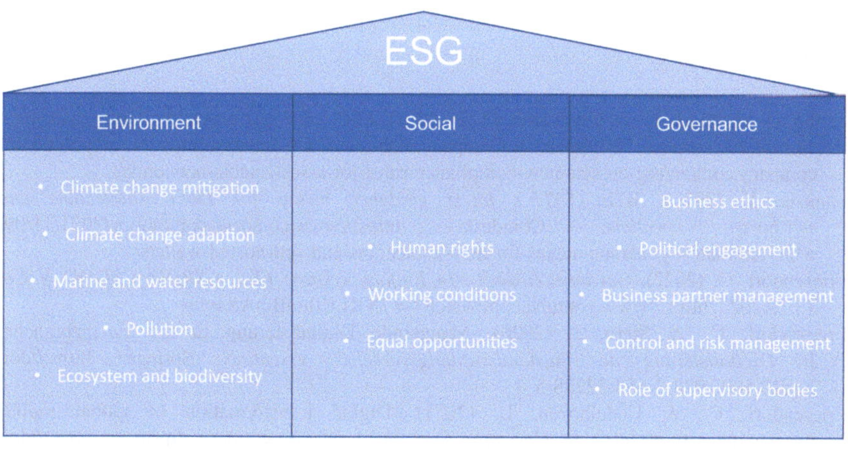

Fig. 7.2 ESG, own illustration

the company. Finally, the governance criteria are concerned with a corporation's audits, leadership, shareholder rights, and executive pay (Erling et al., 2021).

The purpose of the ESG regulation is to develop a more sustainable and greener economy in the EU by accelerating its implementation. ESG is a concept that companies and financial institutions have to follow in order to comply with their responsibilities. A company must qualify its business as sustainable in order for European investors to take notice of their business and invest in it (Friesendorf, 2022).

7.4 Regulatory Transformation

Both DeFi and ESG can reshape the financial industry in a very short period of time. There is a growing interest in new technology and sustainability; in particular, among younger generations. Kane et al. (2021) estimate that ESG ETFs and ESG debt will reach USD 1 trillion and USD 11 trillion by 2025.

In DeFi, early impact projects have been developed, and many projects and platforms are embracing ESG. Specifically, the intersection between ESG and DeFi is going to flourish in the coming years as more institutional capital floods into the DeFi market, which will accelerate innovation (Kisselgof, 2021). It is also important to mention that DeFi will only add value to ESG as a whole. Particularly, the governance criteria are going to improve as DeFi introduces more transparency to the governance process.

As sustainability is one of the most important standards for the younger generation, the symbiotic relationship between ESG and DeFi could have a huge impact on the financial industry. There will therefore be a premium price paid by markets for those companies and systems that create a benefit for the greater good as a result of creating a positive impact on society.

References

Erling, U. M., Stark, C., & Uschkereit, D. T. (2021). *ESG – EU sets new compliance rules for a sustainable economy* | Pohlmann & Company. Pohlmann & Company. https://www.pohlmann-company.com/en/esg-eu-sets-new-compliance-rules-for-a-sustainable-economy/.

Fanusie, Y. (2021). *What FATF's latest guidance means for DeFi, stablecoins and self-hosted wallets*. Coindesk. https://www.coindesk.com/policy/2021/11/09/what-fatfs-latest-guidance-means-for-defi-stablecoins-and-self-hosted-wallets/.

Friesendorf, C. (2022). *Gewinne Zukunft #14 Einfach erklärt: ESG, CSRDD, CSDDD & Co. 13.12.2023*. https://www.youtube.com/watch?v=7NKLCfhmBmA&t=6s

Friesendorf, C., & Stern, J. (2020). Mangelnde Digitalisierung in der Finanzbranche. In *Digitalisierung des Auslandszahlungsverkehrs. essentials*. Springer. https://doi.org/10.1007/978-3-658-32738-5_1

Friesendorf, C., & Uedelhoven, L. (2021). Digital transformation of global mobility markets. In *Mobility in Germany. Springer briefs in business*. Springer. https://doi.org/10.1007/978-3-030-71849-7_1

Friesendorf, C., & Mir Haschemi, N. J. (2023). Private equity in Germany. In *Venture Capital for Digital Platform Start-ups. Springer business guides on the go*. Springer. https://doi.org/10.1007/978-3-031-33708-6

Kane, E., Du Boff, R., Contractor, S., Diab, A., Boucher, M., & Tsang, E. (2021). *BI analyst briefing: Global ESG 2021 midyear outlook* | Bloomberg Professional Services. Bloomberg Professional Services. https://www.bloomberg.com/professional/blog/webinar/bi-analyst-briefing-global-esg-2021-midyear-outlook/

Kisselgof, M. (2021). *ESG DeFi, the next Trillion Dollar Asset Class*. CryptoMode. https://cryptomode.com/esg-defi-the-next-trillion-dollar-asset-class/.

Chapter 8
Comparison of Centralized and Decentralized Finance

8.1 Criterion-Based Tabular Comparison

Decentralized finance is yet an abstract phenomenon that still assumes the precepts and reference to digitalization, digital assets, and thereby represents a radical innovation that is rather the territory of new or unconventional entrepreneurs (Friesendorf & Uedelhoven, 2021; Friesendorf & Mir Haschemi, 2023). Whereas traditional finance is a tried and tested ground where stakeholders aim to incrementally introduce chose aspects of digitalization (Friesendorf & Stern, 2020). When these two juxtaposed philosophies and systems are compared to each other, it is obvious that they are distinct in their own way from our research, we crystallize three kinds of users: (1) the user who operates only in centralized markets, (2) the user who operates only in decentralized markets, and (3) the user who operates in both. Our aim with this chapter is to enable a merging of these behaviors and further enable an easy transition between traditional and decentralized finance.

Table 8.1 illustrates the differences between DeFi and traditional finance based on 11 key factors that differentiate these two types of finance. It is to be noted that a list of factors must be considered in decision-making for any activity in DeFi markets. These include custody of assets, units of accounts, execution, clearing and settlement, governance, auditability, collateral requirements, cross-service interactions, access and privacy, security, and investor protection.

Comparing these key factors with one another, it becomes clear that there are several differences between DeFi and traditional finance that have to be taken into consideration. As compared to traditional finance, DeFi is much more open and transparent. It is possible for anyone who understands the blockchain coding language and is capable of programming in that language to create financial services tools that are based on the blockchain.

C. Friesendorf, A. Blütener, *Decentralized Finance (DeFi)*, Business Guides on the Go, https://doi.org/10.1007/978-3-031-37488-3_8

Table 8.1 Tabular comparison

	DeFi	Traditional finance
Custody of assets	A user can hold their own assets directly through smart contracts or by using noncustodial wallets.	The assets are held by either a regulated financial service provider (for example, a bank) or by a custodian on behalf of the owner of the asset.
Units of account	They are generally denominated in stablecoins or digital assets.	They are denominated in fiat currency.
Execution	It is executed through smart contracts that are implemented on the user's digital assets.	Transactions between parties are typically processed by intermediaries.
Clearing and settlement	Written agreements are used to complete the settlement process.	Clearing and settlement of transactions are usually handled by clearinghouses or service providers after a certain period of time.
Governance	Voting rights are determined by token holders or by protocol developers.	In general, these are defined through the rules and regulations of the marketplace, the service provider, or the self-regulator or regulator.
Auditability	Editors are able to verify activity and protocols using a public ledger and an open-source code.	Third-party audits of proprietary code or open-source code that has been publicly verified.
Collateral requirements	Due to the volatility of digital assets and the absence of a credit score, over-collateralization is typically required.	The collateral required for a transaction is usually equal to or less than the funds provided, or no collateral is required.
Cross-service interaction	It is an open system that integrates any service with other services on the same network/blockchain with the possibility of connecting to multiple chains.	Interaction between services is usually limited. An open finance movement may be achieved through the use of dedicated intermediaries or programmed interfaces.
Access and privacy	Generally, transactions and user balances are available to the public. The AML (anti-money laundering) regulations are currently discussing identity verification.	It is the responsibility of service providers to verify the identity of their users. In spite of this, personal information is protected by national privacy laws.
Security	Generally vulnerable to operational, technical, and other hacks or exploitations.	It is also vulnerable to data breaches and hacks of software systems that control assets.
Investor protection	The DeFi insurance offers protection against losses, but in general, all users assume every risk as a default.	In addition to consumer protections, exposure limits, insurance, anti-fraud schemes, and government-mandated disclosures, investors are also protected.

Source: Based on Gogol et al. (2021)

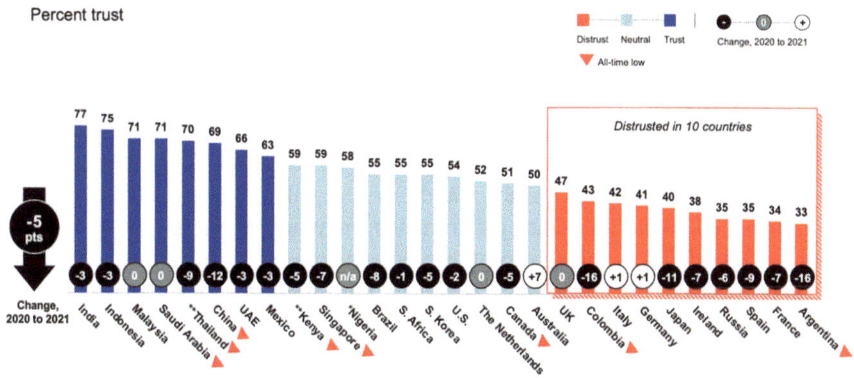

Fig. 8.1 Edelman Trust Barometer Financial Services, own illustration

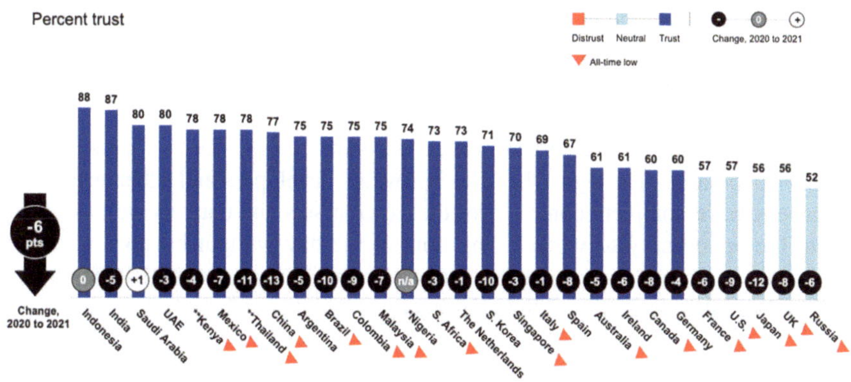

Fig. 8.2 Edelman Trust Barometer Technology

Traditional financial institutions have been working to rebuild client trust in the area of trust and governance. Based on the Edelman Trust Barometer, which is illustrated in Fig. 8.1, this attempt has not been successful yet.

Figure 8.1 illustrates the fact that there is a great deal of mistrust toward the financial services industry in ten major countries. Over the years, the level of distrust toward the European Union has been increasing, especially in European countries. As a comparison, the Edelman Trust Barometer for technology is much higher, with no countries showing a complete distrust regarding technology, even though the trust has declined in the last year as a result of the pandemic (see Edelman, 2021). Figure 8.2 highlights the results of the Edelman study with a special focus on the level of trust with respect to technology.

8.2 Scope of Differences

There is a difference between financial institutions that are regulated by the law and DeFi applications that are regulated by the users who hold the majority of tokens in the network. Due to the fact that DeFi applications are managed by people within the network, there is a good chance that the system will be more trusted than traditional financial institutions since governments and other regulatory agencies are in charge of traditional financial institutions. When people do not trust the government in countries where the government is already untrustworthy, they also do not trust the financial institutions in those countries.

Another important difference between DeFi and traditional finance is the number of entry barriers that are involved. In comparison to traditional finance, DeFi has much fewer entry barriers compared with traditional finance, which is one of the major advantages. Licensing and authorization from regulatory bodies are some of the barriers that need to be overcome. As a result, traditional institutes are left with only a limited scope for the introduction of new innovations (Blockonomist, 2021). Consequently, traditional financial institutions have been burdened by bureaucracy for several years.

As an alternative to traditional finance, decentralized finance has gained a great deal of popularity. Through DLT, DeFi provides developers and other people the chance to have complete control over their own assets and data, as well as giving them the opportunity to work at any time of the day without having to wait on approvals or restrictions to innovate the new financial instruments (Blockonomist, 2021). DeFi therefore allows digital assets to be handled without restriction.

References

Blockonomist. (2021). *Decentralized Finance (DeFi) vs Traditional Payment Institutions. Medium.* https://medium.com/geekculture/decentralized-finance-defi-vs-traditional-payment-institutions-21529873c424

Edelman. (2021). *Edelman Trust Barometer 2021 Technology Sector*. Edelman. https://www.edelman.com/sites/g/files/aatuss191/files/2021-03/2021 Edelman Trust Barometer Tech Sector Report_0.pdf.

Friesendorf, C., & Stern, J. (2020). Mangelnde Digitalisierung in der Finanzbranche. In *Digitalisierung des Auslandszahlungsverkehrs. essentials*. Springer. https://doi.org/10.1007/978-3-658-32738-5_1

Friesendorf, C., & Uedelhoven, L. (2021). Digital transformation of global mobility markets. In *Mobility in Germany. Springer briefs in business*. Springer. https://doi.org/10.1007/978-3-030-71849-7_1

Friesendorf, C., & Mir Haschemi, N. J. (2023). Private equity in Germany. In *Venture Capital for Digital Platform Start-ups. Springer business guides on the go*. Springer. https://doi.org/10.1007/978-3-031-33708-6

Gogel, D., Baker-Taylor, T., Cloots, A. S., Forster, B., Lazaro, J., Schär, F., & Sokolin, L. (2021, May). *DeFi beyond the hype*. The Wharton School. https://wifpr.wharton.upenn.edu/wp-content/uploads/2021/05/DeFi-Beyond-the-Hype.pdf.

Chapter 9
Decentralized Finance: Use-Cases

9.1 Decentralized Stablecoins

The digital economy requires functioning digital products that enable transactions and digital assets that enable the formation of wealth. Together digital platforms and stakeholders could progressively create digital transactions (Friesendorf & Mir Haschemi, 2023). The use of stablecoins is of great importance to DeFi as they reduce the risk associated with highly volatile digital assets. In order to have a functioning value exchange and also to provide investors with a regular income, it is essential to have stable prices (Friesendorf & Stern, 2020; Friesendorf & Uedelhoven, 2021). There is a significant difference between stablecoins that are centralized and stablecoins that are decentralized. Figure 9.1 presents the differences.

There are three types of stablecoins that can be distinguished, such as custodial stablecoins, asset-backed stablecoins, and algorithmic stablecoins.

9.1.1 Custodial Stablecoins

This is because custody stablecoins are centralized stablecoins that use high-quality assets or fiat currency holdings as reserves in order to maintain their value. The instruments do not qualify as DeFi instruments since they require the trust of a custodian to operate. An example of a custodian stablecoin is Diem, the stablecoin that was proposed by Facebook in the form of a stablecoin. In spite of the fact that these stablecoins are not DeFi instruments, they can still be incorporated into DeFi services. The first centralized stablecoin that was introduced was Tether (USDT) (CoinGecko et al., 2020), which was one of the first stablecoins that have been introduced. It is imperative to note that each USDT was backed by 1 USD that was held in the bank account of the issuer. However, there is a significant downside to

C. Friesendorf, A. Blütener, *Decentralized Finance (DeFi)*, Business Guides on the Go, https://doi.org/10.1007/978-3-031-37488-3_9

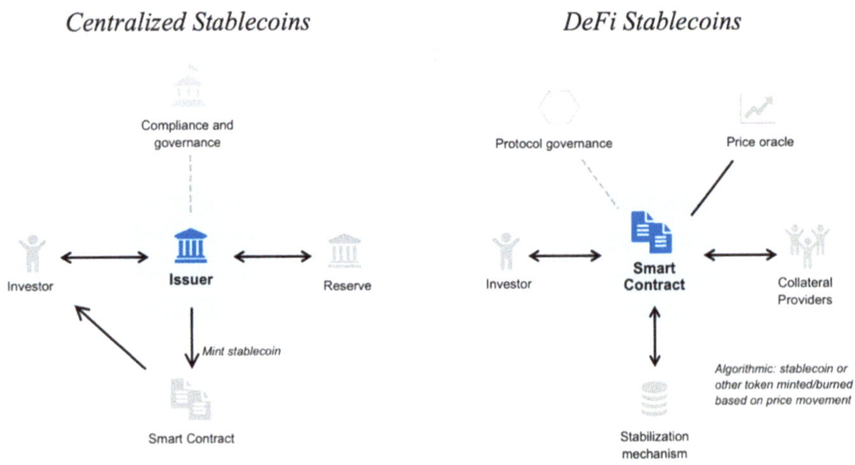

Fig. 9.1 Use-case stablecoins

USDT in that the user has to trust that the reserve exists and that it is fully collateralized, which is a significant disadvantage. It is the aim of the decentralized stablecoins (which belong to the second and third categories) to solve the problem.

9.1.2 *Asset-Backed Stablecoins*

A second category of stablecoins is asset-backed stablecoins, which utilize smart contracts in order to liquidate and assemble collaterals such as cryptocurrencies in order to make the coins more stable.

9.1.3 *Algorithmic Stablecoins*

In order to maintain the peg of cryptocurrency over time, a third category of stablecoins has been developed, namely algorithmic stablecoins, which take advantage of both contraction of the supply and dynamic expansion of digital assets to keep the peg. The two types of stablecoins, algorithmic and asset-backed, are both considered to be DeFi instruments themselves because they operate on a trust-minimized, decentralized, and noncustodial basis, and they operate in a trust-minimized, decentralized, and noncustodial manner.

Over-collateralization is the method used in order to create these stablecoins, which operate on the decentralized ledger completely as they use the over-collateralization method. In addition, there is the possibility that each and every member of the network will be able to audit the reserves of the decentralized stablecoins in a public manner once the network is up and running. Currently, there are decentralized autonomous organizations that are responsible for governance (Hayes, 2022). Stablecoins are not financial applications, but they are valuable to the DeFi movement because they are able to make dApps more accessible to everyone by preserving their value in a stable manner.

9.2 Decentralized Exchanges

It is of utmost importance for the DeFi movement that decentralized exchanges are of great importance since they allow users and holders of different digital assets to access and use DeFi products and services. Furthermore, it is possible for users to generate a profit from the use of their tokens as well.

Figure 9.2 shows the significant differences between centralized and decentralized exchanges.

As a trader, it is imperative to trust the operator of a centralized exchange to keep the funds of his clients safe, settle transactions, match buyers with sellers, and provide accurate pricing information to his clients. It is possible to trade on several different exchanges. It is a good idea to trade fiat-based assets on the NASDAQ (in the USA) or Eurex (in Germany), Coinbase is a good option for trading fiat currency with cryptocurrencies, and Uniswap is a good option for trading only digital assets. In spite of the fact that centralized exchanges are able to exchange cryptocurrencies for the purpose of using DeFi services, they are not programmable nor are they trusted because they are custodial.

Conversely, decentralized exchanges, on the other hand, are programmable and can be accessed through the use of noncustodial wallets. A decentralized exchange is a platform where all transactions are automated and processed by smart contracts.

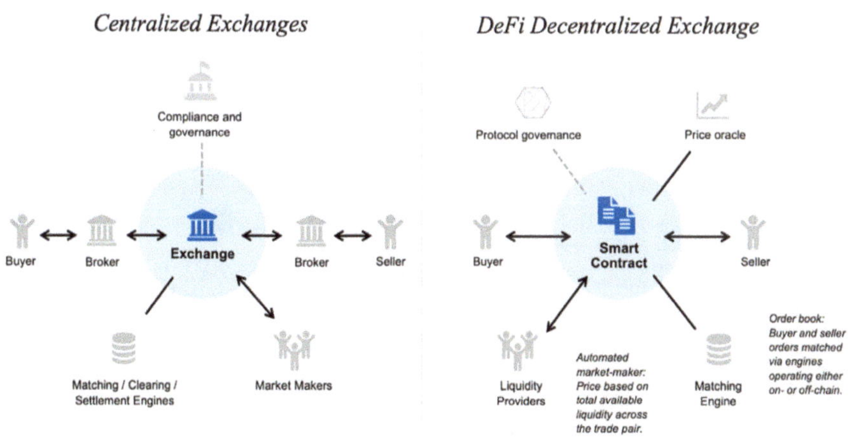

Fig. 9.2 Use-case exchange

It is possible that any user holding digital assets has the option of locking up his funds so that he can earn a yield that is paid by traders or can be used as liquidity for future trades in the marketplace (Gogel et al., 2021).

Rather than having to deal with a list of clients and counterparties that are subject to the bid/ask spread, a trader instead deals with liquidity pools that are being supplied by automated market makers, or AMMs for short.

Uniswap and Sushiswap are the two most prominent decentralized exchanges that are currently being used by the community. As a decentralized AMM protocol built on Ethereum, UniSwap uses algorithms that identify the pool token count of two different currencies that are traded, with the expectation that this count should be equal to a constant (Mihajlovic, 2022). It is important to understand that when tokens are purchased, they are removed from the pool, which results in a hike in their prices in order to maintain a constant value for the tokens. Uniswap's software was used by an unknown developer to create Sushiswap in 2020. In addition, he added a governance token called SUSHI, which allows holders to vote on future exchange changes. Having a right to say in platforms that they are involved in has sparked interest in the exchange, as people are more interested in having a say in platforms they are involved in (Weston, 2022).

9.3 Decentralized Credit

Borrowing and lending are two of the most important parts of financial services. It is important to note that in the centralized version, banks are responsible for determining which assets are liquid, which interest rates are going to be paid to a depositor, and what rates they are going to receive from borrowers on a long-term loan. It also evaluates the credit score of the borrower, as well as his creditworthiness, and

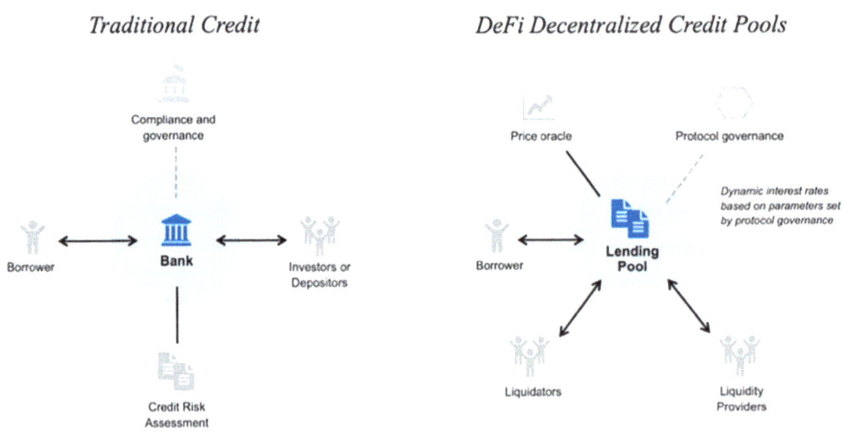

Fig. 9.3 Use-case credit

then establishes an appropriate interest rate based on the borrower's credit score and creditworthiness.

Figure 9.3 illustrates the differences between traditional credit and the DeFi decentralized credit pools.

As opposed to the traditional form of credit, DeFi pools tokens together that are subject to interest rates depending on how many tokens are borrowed compared to how many tokens are supplied. The two most prominent credit protocols are Aaave and Compound. It is by using these protocols that lenders are able to commit their funds to the credit services and will receive tokens and an interest rate in return for doing so. It is lenders who receive the interest rate, and it is borrowers who pay it. During the course of the relationship, both parties have full custody of their own assets, and both parties are capable of liquidating them at any time they wish. In addition to this, decentralized credit is able to circumvent bureaucracy that is usually a burden in traditional lending institutions because the loan and the assets are locked in a smart contract, so there is no need to conduct a borrower evaluation (as in checking their credit score) or any other relevant credit checks.

It is also possible to obtain flash loans through decentralized credit pools. With the help of popular credit protocols such as Aave or dYdX, it is possible to borrow these flash loans instantly. Additionally, they do not require any collateral as long as the liquidity is repaid at the end of the same transaction as it was provided.

In addition to what has already been discussed in previous chapters, decentralized credit pools could remove the barrier to accessing credit for those who are unbanked and allow anyone to receive a loan by pledging their digital assets against the loan. Consequently, decentralized credit opens up a plethora of possibilities for anyone without the need for a bank account in order to take advantage of its benefits.

9.4 Decentralized Derivatives

Derivatives are not just about lending and borrowing but also about creating new risks and developing new opportunities in the market. They also enable financial market transactions to become more sophisticated. It has been described in previous chapters that a derivative is a financial instrument that is based on an underlying asset, a real-world event such as a sports event (prediction market) or the cash flow of an organization (crowdfunding relationship) (Gogel et al., 2021). DeFi decentralized derivatives are different from traditional derivatives in that they are decentralized, as can be seen in Fig. 9.4.

To buy or sell options or futures contracts in traditional finance, the trader typically relies on intermediaries such as commission merchants to help them buy or sell contracts. In addition to that, they also accept assets or money from their clients in order to support these orders. Once the orders are received by the clearing member institutes, the next step is to approve the orders on behalf of the trader by the clearing member institutes. Clearinghouses serve as a middleman between clearing firms, and the legal counterparty risks are assumed by them. By the end of the day,

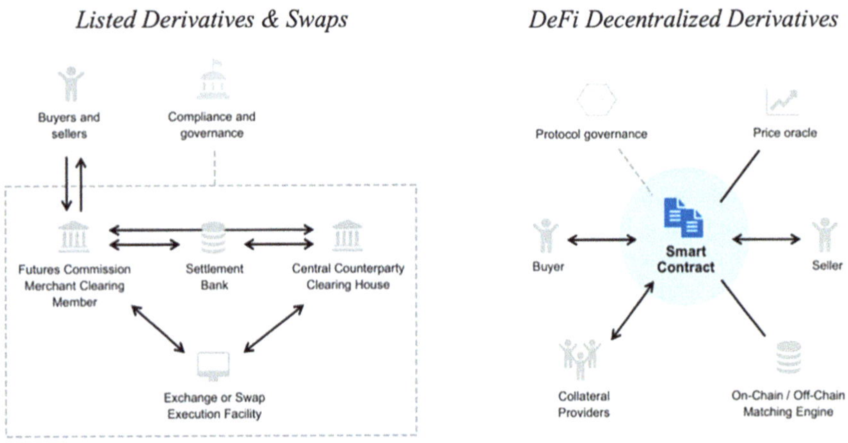

Fig. 9.4 Use-case derivatives

the clearinghouse is involved in all the activities of the trade, such as securing and clearing securities. In addition to the settlement of the trade, the clearinghouse is also responsible for the settlement of the trade.

Unlike the traditional process of trading derivatives, DeFi directly connects sellers and buyers and sets up a collateral pool to back up the trades just like all the other DeFi services. It is possible for some protocols to allow users to purchase and sell synthetic exposure to cryptocurrencies, even if they do not actually hold any of them themselves. There are other dApps that make use of prediction markets. A user may place a wager on the outcome of an event in the future.

On the Ethereum blockchain, Synthetix is a commonly used DeFi protocol for decentralized derivatives. This protocol allows users to receive price exposures to currencies, digital assets, stocks, and commodities through the creation of synthetic assets, which are called Synths. Synths are overcollateralized derivatives that enable users to earn trading fees and participate in governance protocols. In addition, they are able to track the value of assets that a user cannot directly acquire due to regulatory restrictions.

9.5 Decentralized Insurance

DeFi can also be used in the insurance industry as a real-world application. The financial services industry is one of the most risk-averse industries in the world. People who take risks usually benefit from higher profits since they are more likely to take risks. The average investor, however, prefers to pay a small amount in order to prevent more significant losses from occurring in the future. In Fig. 9.5, we

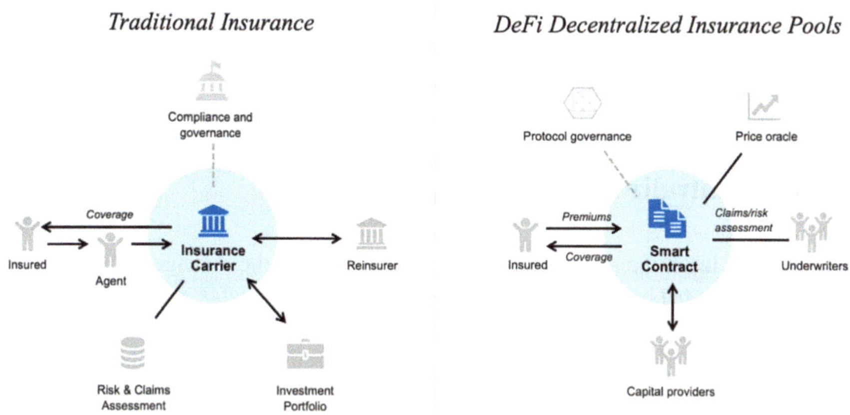

Fig. 9.5 Use-case insurance

present an overview of the differences between the traditional insurance system and the DeFi decentralized insurance pools, as well as their advantages and disadvantages.

The traditional, centralized insurance system to maintain a sufficient amount of funds to pay claims from their clients requires an insurance carrier to balance the premiums they receive against the investments they make in order to maintain a sufficient amount of funds to pay claims from their clients. In addition, the carrier is also responsible for assessing the risk of the client, managing claims, and underwriting the policy.

In addition to the fact that DeFi is able to cover certain financial risks through DeFi derivatives, its greatest opportunity lies in insuring DeFi-related risks such as the failure of smart contracts, game-theoretic risk, and successful hacks of protocols. There is currently no way to insure risks other than those related to financial risks over the DeFi platforms in terms of insurance. Consequently, there is no use-case for insuring a house or the life of the user over a DeFi protocol at this time.

Similarly to other DeFi protocols, DeFi insurance pools are also collateralized with (digital) assets in order to provide the capital that is associated with them in order to provide the benefits associated with them. These pools are capable of reimbursing premium-paying users for their losses in the event that an event occurs where the user needs to be reimbursed for his loss. It is generally the case that claim payments are imposed through token-driven incentives. Usually, before a claim is paid out, there are claim accessors who vote on whether or not the claim will be paid out.

It is called Nexus Mutual, and it is one of the most prominent networks for decentralized insurance that helps users share their DeFi-related risks without having to go through a traditional insurance company in order to share these risks. It is based on the Ethereum blockchain, which is the basis for this network. Currently, Nexus Mutual offers its clients an insurance plan for smart contracts, where the user is required to pay a minimum of 2.6% a year in order to be protected against the risks associated with smart contracts (such as smart contract bugs) (Gogel et al., 2021).

9.6 Decentralized Asset Management

Last but not least, the sixth current use-case for DeFi is the management of assets. According to what has already been stated, asset management is a way of managing a portfolio of assets to be able to generate profits from them in the future. In the case of a fund manager, they will assemble a financial product that is regulated, such as an ETF, mutual fund, private equity interest, or a separately managed account. It is from here that a wealth manager will package the products for asset allocations that are then distributed to the client through brokers and financial advisors (Gogel et al., 2021).

A Robo-Advisor is also able to manage a client's portfolio by providing automated financial services to the client without any human involvement or oversight for the client. The downside of asset management services is that they often come with relatively high service fees, such as hourly fees, plan-by-plan fees, flat fees, and other fees associated with the services provided by financial advisors. DeFi asset management differs from traditional asset management in a number of ways, as presented in Fig. 9.6.

The majority of investments in decentralized asset management consist of tokens, synthetically structured tokens, and traditional exposure is captured by digital assets and interest-generating accounts, all of which are backed by digital assets. Using the protocols of decentralized asset management, these investments can be combined

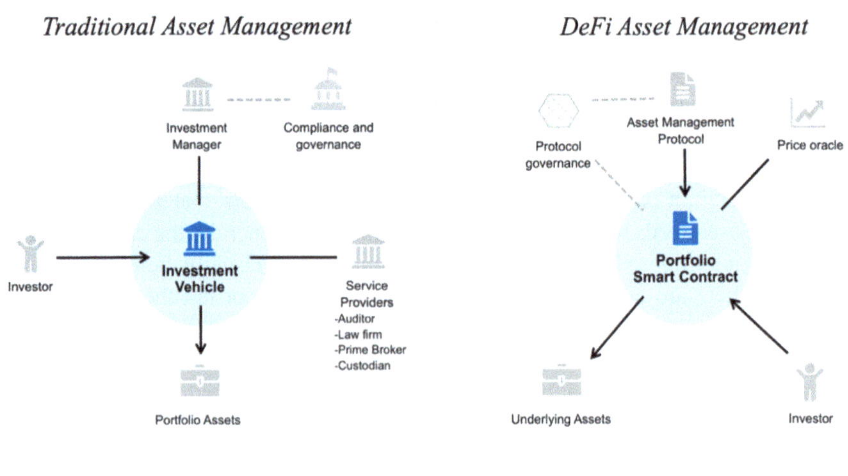

Fig. 9.6 Use-case asset management

through smart contracts into pools or vaults so that they can be managed as decentralized assets. There are currently no boundaries between the package types and asset classes, and the business models for decentralized asset management are still in the process of being developed. The Set Protocol, however, has already been established as an asset management protocol. It enables its users to create tokens that are fully representative of collateralized portfolios consisting of Ethereum, stablecoins, Bitcoin, and other digital assets. Just as with a Robo-Advisor, this protocol will rebalance according to a predefined logic (set by the user).

References

CoinGecko, L., Lau, D., Jin, T. S., Kho, K., Azmi, E., Lee, T., & Ong, B. (2020). *How to DeFi: Beginner* (1st ed.). Independently Published.

Friesendorf, C., & Stern, J. (2020). Mangelnde Digitalisierung in der Finanzbranche. In *Digitalisierung des Auslandszahlungsverkehrs. essentials*. Springer. https://doi.org/10.1007/978-3-658-32738-5_1

Friesendorf, C., & Uedelhoven, L. (2021). Digital transformation of global mobility markets. In *Mobility in Germany. Springer briefs in business*. Springer. https://doi.org/10.1007/978-3-030-71849-7_1

Friesendorf, C., & Mir Haschemi, N. J. (2023). Private equity in Germany. In *Venture Capital for Digital Platform Start-ups. Springer business guides on the go*. Springer. https://doi.org/10.1007/978-3-031-33708-6

Gogel, D., Baker-Taylor, T., Cloots, A. S., Forster, B., Lazaro, J., Schär, F., & Sokolin, L. (2021, May). *DeFi beyond the hype*. The Wharton School. https://wifpr.wharton.upenn.edu/wp-content/uploads/2021/05/DeFi-Beyond-the-Hype.pdf.

Hayes, A. (2022). *Stablecoin definition*. Investopedia. https://www.investopedia.com/terms/s/stablecoin.asp.

Mihajlovic, M. (2022). *What is an AMM (Automated Market Maker) | A beginner's guide to Decentralized Finance (DeFi)*. Shrimpy Academy. https://academy.shrimpy.io/lesson/what-is-an-amm-automated-market-maker

Weston, G. (2022). *Uniswap vs SushiSwap - Key differences*. 101 Blockchains. https://101blockchains.com/uniswap-vs-sushiswap/

Chapter 10
Decentralized Finance: Empirical Analysis of Customer Willingness

10.1 Appraisal of the Qualitative Approach

For this book to provide a basis in decentralized finance (DeFi), which is a young and upcoming instrument and field of work, we conducted a detailed literature review collecting studies and research done qualitatively on a global scale. As compared to business and economics, a qualitative approach in empirical methods plays a predominant role in social sciences, especially in social life, wherein qualitative research serves as an umbrella term for a variety of approaches that have been adapted over the past years.

In this book, we have collected and presented information of a qualitative nature, which can be further broken down to or assigned to a variety of textual materials, such as documents, Internet sites, field notes, video recordings, and transcripts of interviews (Saldaña, 2011). The primary advantage of using qualitative data in research is that readers or the research audience are able to experience the chronological flow, cause-and-effect phenomenon from the listing of the consequences, and the incidents or events that triggered a result or a response, which varies on the scale of expectation of the researcher.

An added advantage is that a good qualitative study is capable of leading into the discovery of unknown influential factors, which require integration and scaling of the study, thereby helping the researcher to revise the conceptual framework and prepare a better fit by accounting for and integrating new data (Friesendorf & Uedelhoven, 2021; Miles & Huberman, 1994). Our goal during this exercise of literature collection and review was to provide a comprehensive overview of the status quo of the DeFi movement. As part of this process, our subgoals were to identify the events and factors that have thus far shaped the financial sector into what we know of today. For this purpose, our literature review undertook an assessment of the scientific studies and investigated discussions and debates on online forums such as trending online blogs and platforms like Reddit, especially on the topics of

C. Friesendorf, A. Blütener, *Decentralized Finance (DeFi)*, Business Guides on the Go, https://doi.org/10.1007/978-3-031-37488-3_10

blockchain, cryptocurrencies, and DeFi, to get a realistic idea of the number of participants on these topics as well as the volume of knowledge on this field in the practitioner area.

There was one helpful platform that we used, and that was IOHK (Input Output Hong Kong), which is a leading research and engineering platform for cryptography. Due to the fact that this is a relatively new field, it is hard to find books or other similar materials outside of the Internet when it comes to DeFi. Consequently, most of the material can be found on the Internet in forums, blogs, or social networks like Discord, YouTube, or Twitter, all of which can be found on the Internet. The use of Google Scholar provided more research-based papers by using keywords such as DeFi, decentralized finance, Blockchain, Ethereum, banking, status quo of banking, decentralized technologies, DeFi use-cases, Bitcoin, DTL, financial industry trust, stablecoins, DAO, AMM, smart contracts, EZB, banking license, and competitors in the banking industry as well.

10.2 Hypothesis-Building and Validation

In order to validate the hypotheses, we considered in the previous sections that form an exhaustive literature review on various decentralized finance (DeFi) options, we deemed it necessary and sufficient to conduct an online survey that sought detailed answers to our proposals on implementing DeFi. The use of surveys is a common method of gathering sample data from individuals and is generally a set of questions that have a range of answers from which individuals can choose. Furthermore, by using surveys, a large amount of data can be relatively structured and standardized for each case, which helps the researcher to understand a population or a target group or a milieu, as a whole.

The survey was conducted via survio.com. Survio is an online platform that helps its users to create online surveys such as employee feedback, customer satisfaction, and market research, quickly and efficiently. Participants were able to access the survey over a direct link that was shared on prominent social media platforms such as Instagram, Facebook, LinkedIn, and Xing. Additionally, the link for the survey was sent over the popular messenger application WhatsApp to friends, colleagues, and relatives.

As part of the survey, the target group of this survey consisted of Europeans of all ages, with the requirements that they had basic financial knowledge and a bank account as a condition for participation. We formulated a set of 15 questions in the survey, and we made it available online for three weeks, starting on February 21, 2022, and ending on March 14, 2022.

Participants were required to acknowledge at the beginning of the survey that the survey was solely designed to gather data for research on DeFi. Additionally, the survey was completely anonymous, and the participant had the option to end the survey at any time. We refer to the participant using the male form for ease of use. Our survey participants were of diverse ages and gender.

In the first section of the survey, in questions 1 to 4, the participants were asked to identify their generation. Having this demographic question enabled us to filter the different age groups according to their investment preferences. We then asked the participants three questions about their satisfaction level with their bank, if they would recommend it to their friends and family, and the reason why they would not recommend it to them. The purpose of these questions was to allow the participants to get a sense of how they feel about their own bank and about traditional banks in general.

The second group of questions, from 5 to 7, and 13 to 14, were designed to deal with sustainability and the ESG requirements that are at the forefront in financial and investment branches. These questions were formulated to find out information and determine whether the participants trusted their bank to adhere to these standards and also to find out from them an overview of which banks they considered to be the most sustainable.

In the third section of the questionnaire, namely questions 8, 9, and 12, the participants were asked about their attitudes regarding entrepreneurship and their willingness to change the current financial system. Lastly, questions 10, 11, and 15 were designed to determine the participants' investment behavior and their attitude toward volatile investments, to be specific, cryptocurrencies. During the administration of the online survey, we anticipated a maximum of 100 participants and a minimum of 20 to be able to carry out a meaningful analysis of the survey results.

Gathering the results of the online survey, we summarize these in the next sections on the basis ranging from the most interesting to the most problematic aspects of DeFi so as to derive a hypothesis that can explain the future of DeFi.

10.3 Survey Questions and Results

Our survey participants answered 15 questions concerning the overall financial sector beginning by giving information about themselves to enable us to get an idea of the customer profile.

10.3.1 Customer Age Demographics

In the first section, the participants were asked to select which generation, according to their birth year, they belong to in order to be able to receive a more in-depth understanding of and analysis of the answers they made to the survey. Figure 10.1 illustrates the age demographic of all participants.

Millennials (58 out of 150 participants) were the age group with the most participants in the online survey, followed by Generation Z (37), Baby Boomers (32), and Generation X (23).

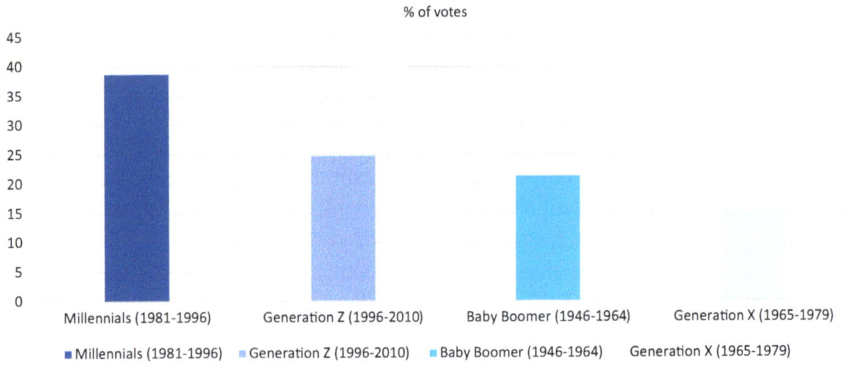

Fig. 10.1 Which generation do you belong to?

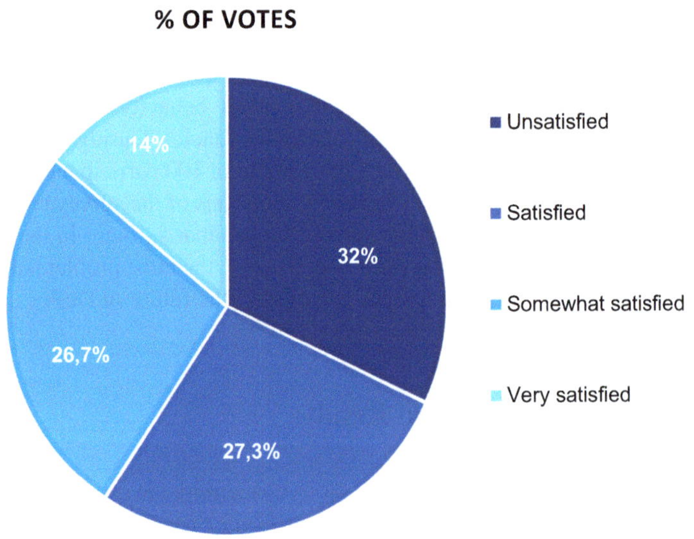

Fig. 10.2 How satisfied are you with your bank?

10.3.2 Generational Satisfaction with Their Bank

On a scale from unsatisfied to extremely satisfied, participants were asked whether they were currently satisfied with their banks. Figure 10.2 illustrates the results in terms of percentage based on generation.

Figure 10.3 provides the results of the question in categories of commonly understood generations as baby boomers, Generation X, Millennials, and Generation Y.

Overall, 32% of participants are dissatisfied with their bank. Around 27.3% and 26.7% of participants are satisfied or somewhat satisfied with their experience. Only 14% of participants are very satisfied, and no participant is extremely satisfied. There is potential for further analysis of this result.

	Unsatisfied	Somewhat satisfied	Satisfied	Very Satisfied
Baby Boomer (1946 – 1964)	2	11	13	6
Generation X (1965 – 1979)	12	7	3	1
Millennials (1981 – 1996)	21	13	16	8
Generation Z (1996 – 2010)	13	9	9	6
∑ Total	48	40	41	21

Fig. 10.3 How satisfied are you with their bank? Results in different generations

	Yes	No
Baby Boomer (1946 – 1964)	23	9
Generation X (1965 – 1979)	7	16
Millennials (1981 – 1996)	29	29
Generation Z (1996 – 2010)	18	19
∑ Total	77	73

Fig. 10.4 Would you recommend your bank?

Figure 10.3 shows that the generation of baby boomers are the most satisfied with their current bank. Figure 10.4 establishes this fact further and throws light on the thoughts of the younger generations that are not completely happy with their bank.

As a rule, it seems that the younger generations (Generation Z and Millennials) are unsatisfied with their banks to a greater extent than the older generations, namely Generation X and Baby Boomers.

10.3.3 Bank Recommendation Tendency

A similar result can be seen when looking at the question of whether participants would recommend their bank to friends and family. Figure 10.5 shows that those satisfied with their bank also recommend their bank. In other words, the Millennials and Generation Y are not inclined to recommend their bank following their overall dissatisfaction.

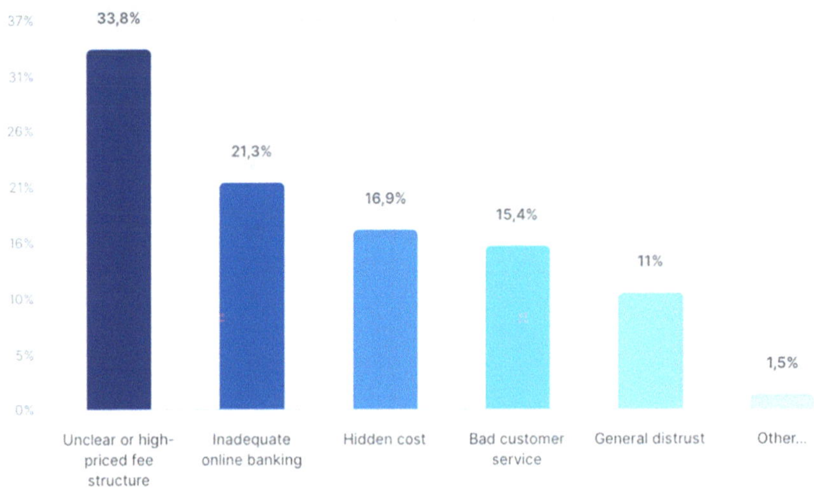

Fig. 10.5 Reasons for a "No"

There is no doubt that the Baby Boomers would recommend their current bank to their friends and family, whereas the Millennials and Gen Z are divided in their opinion on this matter (nearly 50% for no and 50% for yes). There is no doubt that Generation X would not recommend their current banks to their friends and family members. Overall, 51.3% of participants recommended their bank to their friends and family, while 48.7% did not.

10.3.4 Reasons for Not Recommending Their Bank

Figure 10.5 illustrates that out of 48.7% of participants who voted "no," the main reason for not recommending the bank was the unclear or high-priced fee structure, followed by inadequate online banking and hidden fees. Participants were least likely to recommend the bank due to poor customer service and general distrust. According to this result, the fee structure is still not transparent enough to customers, which is one of the main advantages of DeFi that was already discussed in a previous chapter.

10.3.5 Environment, Social, and Governance (ESG) Impact

When it comes to ESG goals, especially sustainability, 50% of all survey participants believe that their banks are not doing enough to achieve social goals, such as becoming more sustainable and transparent, and to increase the level of fairness in their operations. It is estimated that only around 15% of participants agreed that their bank would do enough to achieve ESG goals if the goals were set. As for the remaining 34.7% of respondents, they were unsure whether or not their bank would achieve ESG goals. Figure 10.6 provides a distribution ESG perceptions among respondents.

Over 75% of all participants in the survey don't believe that the top management of their bank is thinking progressively for the bank to become a sustainable financial service provider in the future. There is a belief among the younger generations, specifically Gen Z and Millennials, that the top management of the organization does not think in a progressive manner. Figure 10.7 compares their results between the generations. It is evident from the results that Baby Boomers are much more likely than other generations to trust the top management of an organization.

From the results, it is evident that there are significant differences in the preferences and choices between the generations. It is widely believed that Millennials and Generation Z are the most sustainability-conscious generations to date. Both generations are most likely to make decisions and purchases based on their principles and values (Petro, 2021). In addition, younger generations are much more knowledgeable about how to pick a service provider who aligns with their own principles and values, as well as how to pick a provider that is sustainable based on their own principles and values.

10.3.6 The Value of Sustainability as Progressive or Futuristic

There is no doubt that this shows the results of question six of the survey, in which participants were asked which bank they considered to be sustainable and progressive in their opinion. Figure 10.8 gives information on the perception of sustainable and progressive banks in Germany in the respondents' view.

It is interesting to note that the first three leading banks in the survey results, Tomorrow, N26, and DKB, are all online banks. This means that when compared

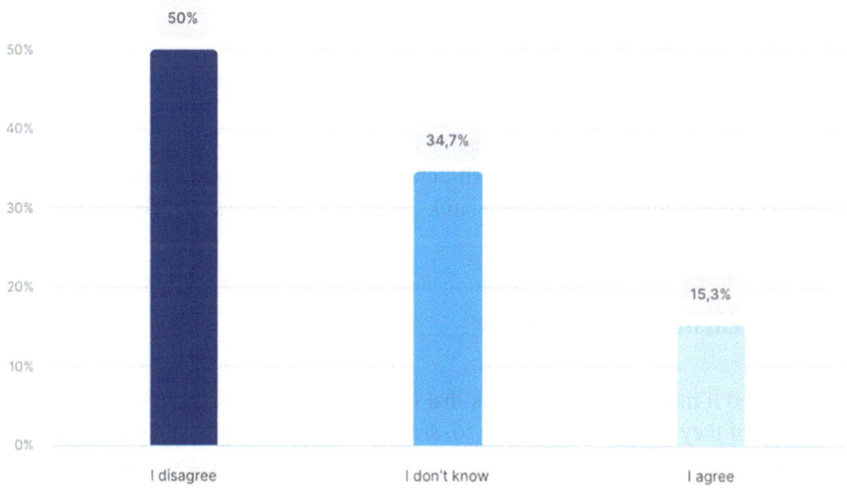

Fig. 10.6 ESG fairness and transparency

	Yes	No
Baby Boomer (1946 – 1964)	13	19
Generation X (1965 – 1979)	5	18
Millennials (1981 – 1996)	10	48
Generation Z (1996 – 2010)	9	28
∑ Total	37	113

Fig. 10.7 ESG results per generation

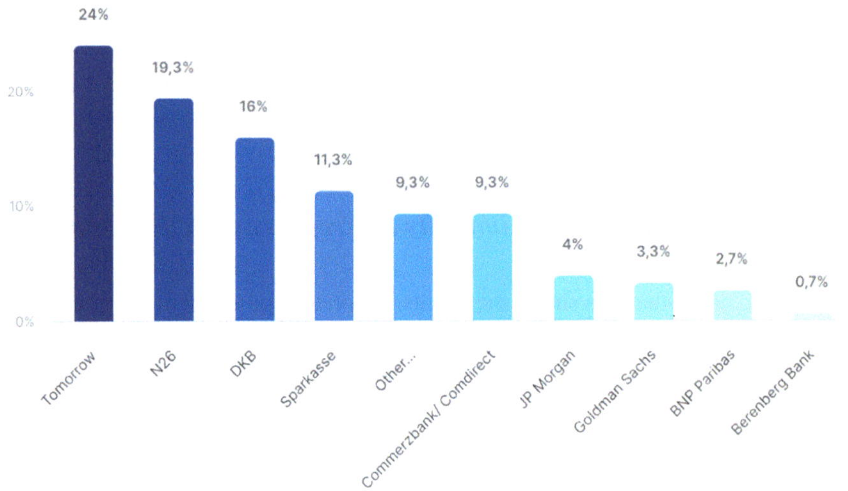

Fig. 10.8 Sustainable and progressive banks in Germany

to other major players in the financial sector, online banks are perceived to be the most progressive financial providers. Taking a closer look at this result, it can also be seen that the younger generations, as against Gen X and Baby Boomers, have voted more often for online banks which contrasts with the older generations who have voted more often for traditional banks. Figure 10.9 illustrates this phenomenon.

10.3.7 Customer as Investor

When asked if they would start a bank that is devoted to technology, equality, and sustainability if they had the assets to do so, around 52% of the participants said that they would do so. In this case, the majority of Gen Z and Gen X have voted in favor of opening their own bank. Baby Boomers are overwhelmingly against the idea of opening their

	Baby Boomer (1946 – 1964)	Generation X (1965 – 1979)	Millennials (1981 – 1996)	Generation Z (1996 – 2010)
N26	2	4	14	9
Tomorrow	4	3	15	14
DKB	4	5	11	4
Goldman Sachs	1	1	2	1
Berenberg Bank	0	1	0	0
BNP Paribas	2	2	0	0
JP Morgan	1	1	4	0
Sparkasse	7	4	4	2
Commerzbank	3	1	4	6
Other	8	1	4	1
∑ Total	32	23	58	37

Fig. 10.9 Listing of German banks perceived as sustainable and progressive

	Yes	No
Baby Boomer (1946 – 1964)	13	19
Generation X (1965 – 1979)	17	6
Millennials (1981 – 1996)	25	33
Generation Z (1996 – 2010)	23	14
∑ Total	78	72

Fig. 10.10 Starting a bank

own bank if they had the assets to do so, and Millennials are torn on the issue as well. There are several differences between the generations, as shown in Fig. 10.10.

It is evident from Figs. 10.10 and 10.11 that the main reason for the decision to open a bank was that the participants felt that the current financial system was unjust and needed to be changed.

Approximately 30% of the people who have expressed interest in opening a bank have stated that, in their opinion, the financial system is unjust, while 23.5% have stated that they would like to make a difference in the world. About 21% of people say that they want to open a bank in order to motivate and inspire others, while 12.7% of people say that they want to open a bank because they have the skills or they are dissatisfied with the bank they are working for at the moment.

We wish to point out that this result highlights and establishes again the Edelman trust barometer that was previously discussed. Due to the fact that all of the participants are from European backgrounds, most of them have serious trust issues toward financial providers, as reflected in the Edelman Trust Barometer. As a result, Gen Z is known for having a higher appetite for risk than previous generations of their

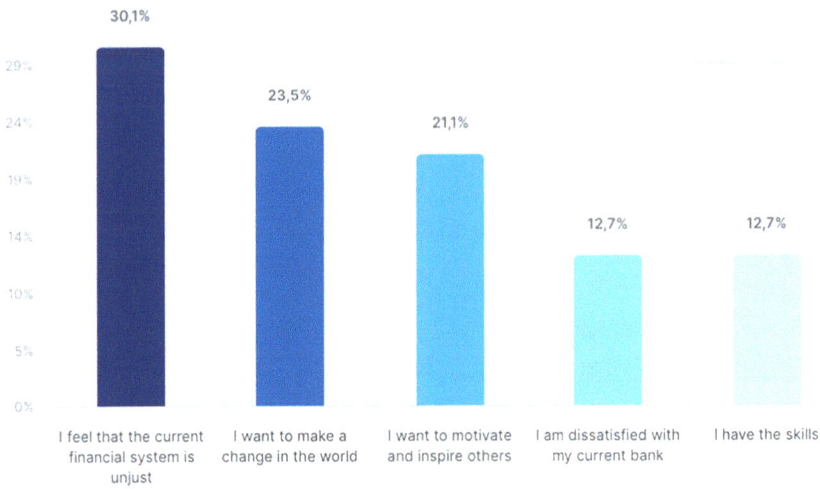

Fig. 10.11 Reasons for starting a bank if one had the assets

generation. As already discussed in the above sections, most Gen Z participants are dissatisfied with their bank, and they do not believe that banks and their management are working toward ESG goals. Having a sense that the current financial system is unfair contributes to dissatisfaction with the current financial system, which is one of the reasons why the younger generation wishes to change it.

There is another reason why the majority of Gen Z has voted to open their own bank is that the generation is very keen on entrepreneurship, which makes them a good candidate to open a bank. As per a recent survey conducted by JA Worldwide and EY Ripple, Gen Z is surveyed as being entrepreneurially minded according to the survey. There are around 53% of participants in the study who have indicated that they would rather run their own business than work for someone else, like their parents or grandparents (Sawyer, 2021). It was also found in the survey that Gen Z members have a high appetite for proactiveness and a strong desire to make a difference at the organizations around them.

About Gen Z

Gen Zers are highly motivated by original ideas, diversity, and problem-solving when it comes to their work lives,

Gen Z is characterized by a high level of confidence and optimism about the future,

There is a tendency for them to view large businesses and primary education as the main sources of information about what their future career paths may look like.

It is clear from these findings that the observations made in this online survey are valid and help us to better understand how the younger generation votes and how they think about financial matters.

10.3.8 Investment Preferences and Behaviors

As far as investing behaviors are concerned, the majority of participants still prefer to invest in conservative investment options like real estate, shares, and bonds when it comes to investing. Taking a look at the following statistics, it can be seen that 32.7% and 25.3% of respondents voted in favor of these investment options. Figure 10.12 illustrates survey participants' preferences for investments.

In spite of this, 24.7% of participants have chosen to invest their money in cryptocurrencies. There is only a 0.6% difference between this investment option and the option of investing in stocks or bonds. There is no doubt that the interest in investing in cryptocurrencies is growing among the general population as a consequence. An example of this can be seen in Fig. 10.13, where participants had the option to invest in ETFs as well.

There was still a preference for the most conservative option among the participants in this study. Despite that, the shares or bonds option was still very closely followed by cryptocurrencies in terms of performance.

Figure 10.14 shows that when it comes to how the different generations have voted on investing in cryptocurrencies, it is clear that the younger generations tend to be the most interested in investing in digital assets. Here we asked the participants if they would have half a million to euros to spend, and if they choose to invest,

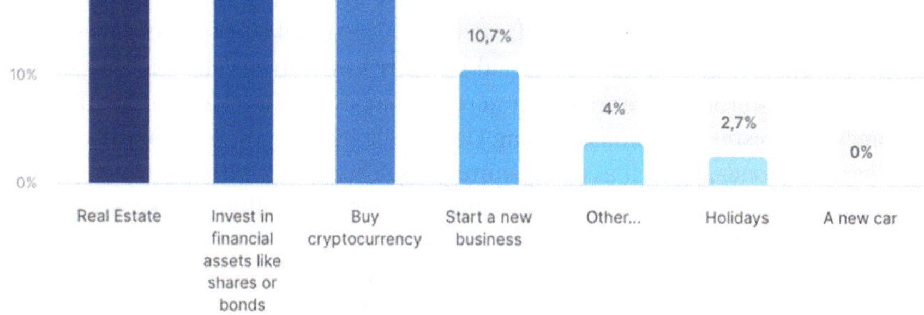

Fig. 10.12 Investment preferences with half a million euros

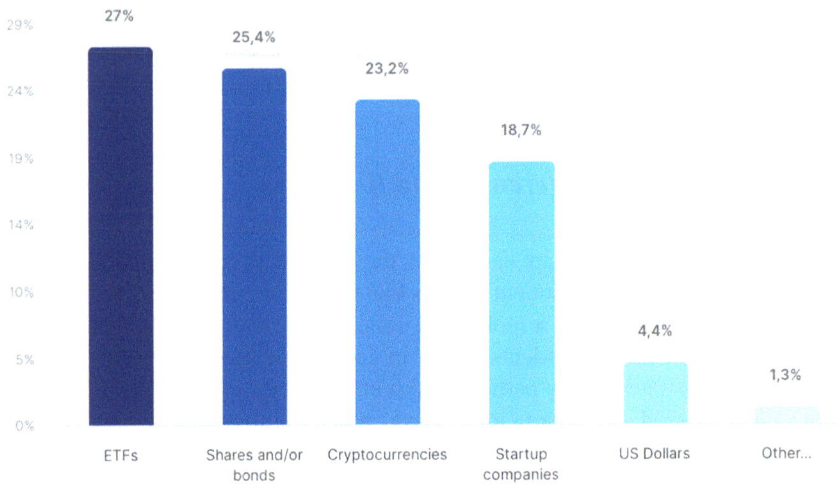

Fig. 10.13 Investment preferences including ETFs

	Baby Boomer (1946 – 1964)	Gen X (1965 – 1979)	Millennials (1981 – 1996)	Gen Z (1996 – 2010)
A new car	0	0	0	0
Start a new business	2	5	6	3
Real Estate	15	5	21	8
Shares or Bonds	11	7	13	7
Cryptocurrency	1	6	14	16
Other	2	0	2	2
∑ Total	32	23	58	37

Fig. 10.14 Investing half a million, results per generation

which financial product or investment option they would consider. The question turned out interesting results from the perspective of risk appetites.

Baby Boomers, on the other hand, are not willing to take the risk of investing in cryptocurrencies because they are afraid of the risks involved. The majority of participants in this group prefer to invest in real estate as well as shares or bonds when it comes to investment options. Among Gen X, the majority of votes have been cast for shares or bonds, as well as cryptocurrencies. There has also been a vote in favor of starting a new business, which shows that they are also willing to take a risk when it comes to investing.

Real estate has been voted by a majority of Millennials, followed by cryptocurrency and shares or bonds as the third most popular choice. While millennials are known to be more risk averse than their younger counterparts, Gen Z, they tend to be more conservative and long-term oriented when it comes to investing. There has been a recent study conducted by Legg Mason which found that millennials are becoming less inclined to take risks, according to the study. A large percentage of this age group hoards cash and is not willing to invest or take a risk as a result of volatile markets. Additionally, the survey has also found that around 85% of American Millennials believe that they should be more conservative when it comes to investing their money when compared to their parents.

In contrast, the youngest generation, known as Gen Z, is far more open to taking risks than the older generations. According to a study by Barclays researchers, 49% of Gen Z investors are making short-term investments. The reason they are willing to take more risks is that they are trying to "get rich quick" with volatile investment options. We will also be able to gain some insight into these perceptions during the course of this survey as part of our analysis of the results of the survey. Several members of Generation Z have voted to invest in cryptocurrencies and open their own banks, according to a recent poll. Consequently, it can be said that Gen Z could become a potential target market for DeFi services in the future.

10.3.9 Zero-Switching Costs Scenario

In the survey, we asked participants about which factors would be the most important that will encourage them to switch their bank at zero costs. Figure 10.15 presents the results of the answers to this question.

Good customer service was rated as the most important factor by participants, followed by corporate social responsibility and sustainability as the second and third most important factors. Fairness was considered to be the least important factor, followed by the bank dealing with high-quality money and the bank's reputation. Figure 10.16 shows how the different generations have voted in this section. It can be seen that all four groups of generations have voted differently on the factors that each group deems to be most important.

There has been a vote by Baby Boomers that all factors are important to them, with the distinction of the cost of services being affordable. As far as Generation X is concerned, sustainability is one of the most important factors, followed by the fact that the bank only deals with high-quality money and that there is no suspicion of money laundering taking place at the bank. It is by far the most important factor for millennials to switch their bank if the customer service is not up to their expectations.

Next in importance are the costs of services and corporate social responsibility. According to Gen Z, corporate social responsibility is the most important factor, followed by all other factors. As a result of these results, it was surprising to find that sustainability did not rank as high in the voting of Gen Z as it usually does for younger generations, despite sustainability being a topic that is usually considered important by them.

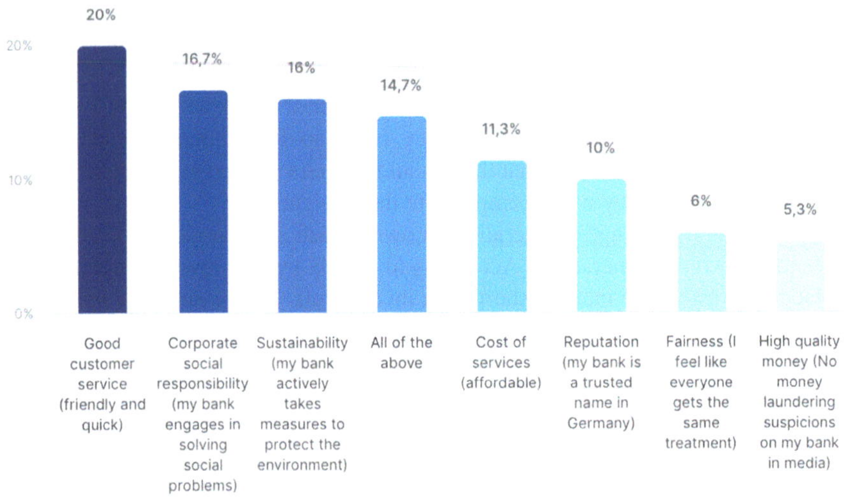

Fig. 10.15 Factors influencing switching to a new bank

	Baby Boomer (1946 – 1964)	Generation X (1965 – 1979)	Millennials (1981 – 1996)	Generation Z (1996 – 2010)
Fairness (I feel like everyone gets the same treatment)	0	1	3	5
High quality money (No money laundering suspicions on my bank in media)	0	4	4	0
Good customer service (friendly and quick)	5	2	19	4
Reputation (my bank is a trusted name in Germany)	4	2	19	4
Sustainability (my bank actively takes measures to protect the environment)	4	5	4	2
Corporate social responsibility (my bank engages in solving social problems)	4	1	8	11
Cost of services (affordable)	6	2	8	1
All of the above	7	3	6	6
∑ Total	32	23	58	37

Fig. 10.16 Factors for switching at zero cost, generational choice

10.3.10 Green Pressure on Banks in Germany

In order to find out the source of customer perception across generations, we raised questions in the survey relating to the political setup in Germany. The green and/or the social parties advocate trust and welfare that may be centrifugal in ESG implementation in Germany. Figure 10.17 shows that a majority of the participants of the survey believe that politics generally puts a lot of pressure on banks to aim for sustainability and progression.

This question on sustainability is critical, especially because, for the first time, there is a combination, i.e., the new German three-party coalition, which was formed in late 2021 by free democrats, social democrats, and greens. This confluence has a very interesting agenda that have conflicting goals on sustainability and economic progress. Our results show many interesting insights.

We see from our survey that 56.7% of participants believed that banks in Germany are under pressure to be more sustainable due to the current coalition government, which is socially, environmentally, and futuristically oriented. However, the difference between the participants who have voted "no" and the participants who have voted "yes" is only 13.4%, which means that the participants are divided in their opinion regarding this decision.

According to the results in Fig. 10.18, it can be seen that there is a clear difference between the younger and older generations of the population when it comes to their perception of how much pressure the new government is putting on the banks.

However, Gen X and Baby Boomers are much more divided when it comes to making this decision. The majority of Baby Boomers have voted that they do not think that the new coalition will put any pressure on banks. The majority of Gen X has voted that they believe that the banks will be put under pressure in the future, while the other half of the generation seems to disagree with that statement.

Every fourth person under the age of 40 who voted in the German election has voted for the green party. Additionally, one in four voters between the ages of 18 and 39 indicated that they wanted a government led by the Green Party. There are only about 21% of those in this age group who would like to see a government led by the Union in power. Over half of all voters over the age of 65 wanted a government led by the SPD. As a result of the projections for the upcoming federal election, the Green Party did not do well, with only 14.4% of the votes projected for the party. As a result of that, it is common for Germany's older voters to prefer the CDU/CSU over the CDU/CSU. As far as voters over the age of 70 are concerned, the Greens are among the worst performers among the major parties.

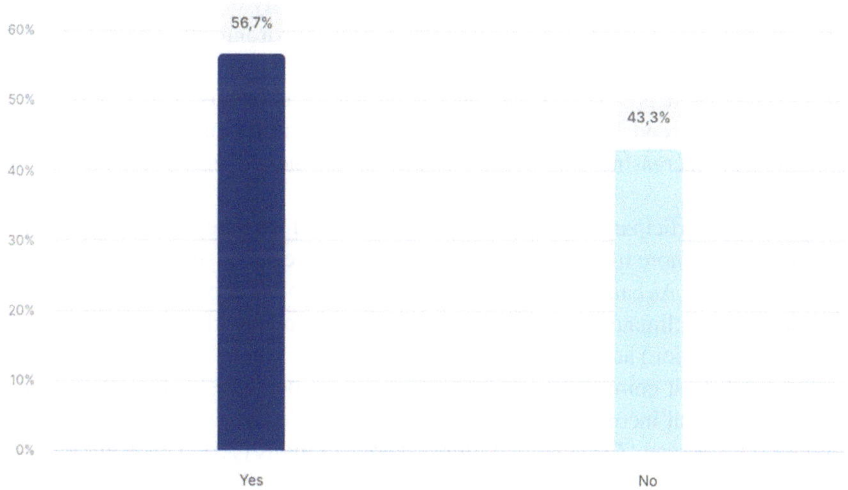

Fig. 10.17 Pressure of green politics on banks in Germany

	Yes	No
Baby Boomer (1946 – 1964)	13	19
Generation X (1965 – 1979)	12	11
Millennials (1981 – 1996)	37	21
Generation Z (1996 – 2010)	23	14
∑ Total	85	65

Fig. 10.18 Pressure on banks, generational views

In this group, only 7% of the voters voted for the Green Party. The AfD (6%) and "Die Linke" (4%) were the only parties with even lower popularity than the AfD. According to, the CDU/CSU scored 39% in this age group, while the SPD scored 34%.

The main reason why the younger generations think that the banks are under more pressure now is because of the new government since the Greens are currently the most popular party among people under 25 years of age. Approximately 23% of the youngest group of voters voted for the Green Party, which puts the party one point ahead of the FDP in terms of the percentage of votes. After that comes the SPD with 14% of the votes. Only about one in ten voters wanted to see the Union in the government. Even so, sustainability remains a prominent topic for younger generations when it comes to the environment.

According to Yamane and Kaneko (2021), the majority of young people prioritize a sustainable environment because they want the environment to be healthy and green in order to be able to have a stable future of their own (Yamane & Kaneko, 2021). Whether it is "Fridays for Future" or other campaigns, sustainability has become a megatrend that is echoing through every sector of the market and is becoming an increasingly important aspect of businesses and everyday life as a whole.

Moreover, participants who voted "yes" were asked why they believe that banks in Germany are more likely to become more sustainable as a result of the new coalition in Germany. As can be seen in Fig. 10.19, the majority of participants voted for weather-related climate disasters (21.8%) and demographic change (for example, an aging population) at 21.3%.

The third most commonly selected reason is irresponsible banks (19.4%), followed by stagnant incomes (18%). One of the least selected reasons is greedy corporates (11.8%) and "Fridays for Future" demonstrations (7.1%), as well as other reasons (0.5%).

10.3.11 Inclination to Cryptocurrency Investments

The last question that was asked was whether the participants would be willing to purchase cryptocurrency if their bank offered it to them, and whether they would be willing to do so. As can be seen in Fig. 10.20, the results are diverse.

In this question, around 58.7% of participants have voted "yes" in response to the question. This is a significant result for the future of DeFi services in the sense that cryptocurrencies have become a vital part of the network as they are the primary means by which DeFi products and services are purchased and paid for. Figure 10.21 gives the distribution of respondent answers indicating that younger generations are more willing to use cryptocurrency.

The results of the answers to the question on cryptocurrency usage vary in a pattern similar to the questions above. There is a higher interest in younger generations to experiment with cryptocurrency. Meaning to say that this referendum, which is a pro-cryptocurrency attitude, was voted for by three generations, Generation X, Millennials, and Generation Z. If their bank offered cryptocurrencies, they would use and buy them as soon as possible. As far as the Baby Boomers were concerned, they were the only ones who have voted "no." Even if their bank offered cryptocurrencies, they would not purchase them. It is readily apparent that the baby boomer generation has a problem with modern digital currencies such as Bitcoin, Ethereum, and Co. This generation prefers stocks to digital assets.

In addition, Harris Poll conducted an online survey of 2000 US adults between 2017 and 2020 about Bitcoin and found similar results. The study indicates that millennials are particularly interested in digital currencies.

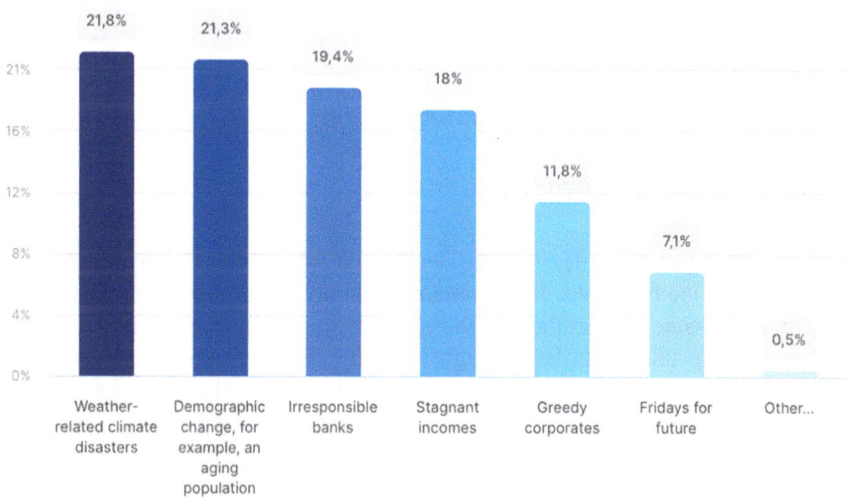

Fig. 10.19 Reasons for pressure on banks

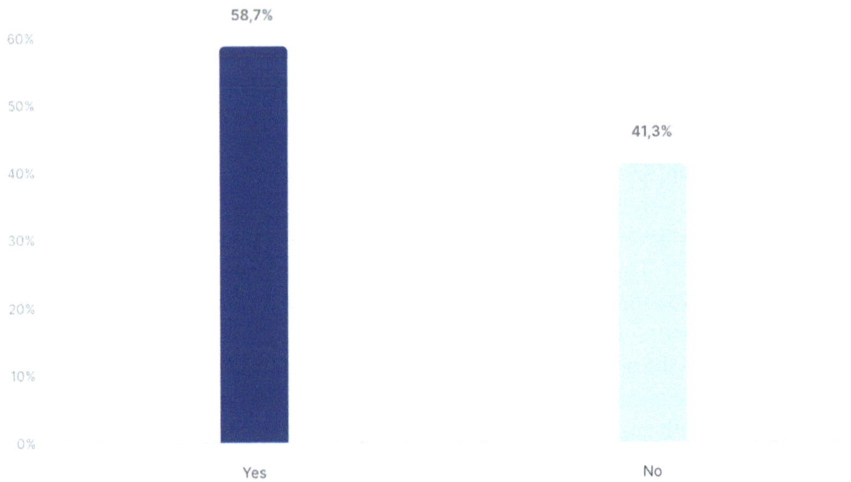

Fig. 10.20 Willingness to purchase cryptocurrency offered by home-bank

	Yes	No	∑ Total
Baby Boomer (1946 – 1964)	6	26	32
Generation X (1965 – 1979)	17	6	23
Millennials (1981 – 1996)	35	23	58
Generation Z (1996 – 2010)	30	7	37
∑ Total	88	62	150

Fig. 10.21 Cryptocurrency usage as per generation

10.3.12 Place of Bitcoin

Around 27% of Millennials even consider Bitcoin to be a more trustworthy form of payment than the big banks. It is estimated that only 8% of those over 65 years of age share the same view as those in the younger generation (Bogart, 2020). One of the reasons for this might be the high volatility and risk associated with digital assets. As a result, there is also a possibility that the concept of digital assets may be too abstract for older people to understand. Nevertheless, there has been an increase in the likelihood of buying digital assets, such as Bitcoin, over the years, regardless of one's age. Figure 10.22 illustrates the propensity of customers to use Bitcoin.

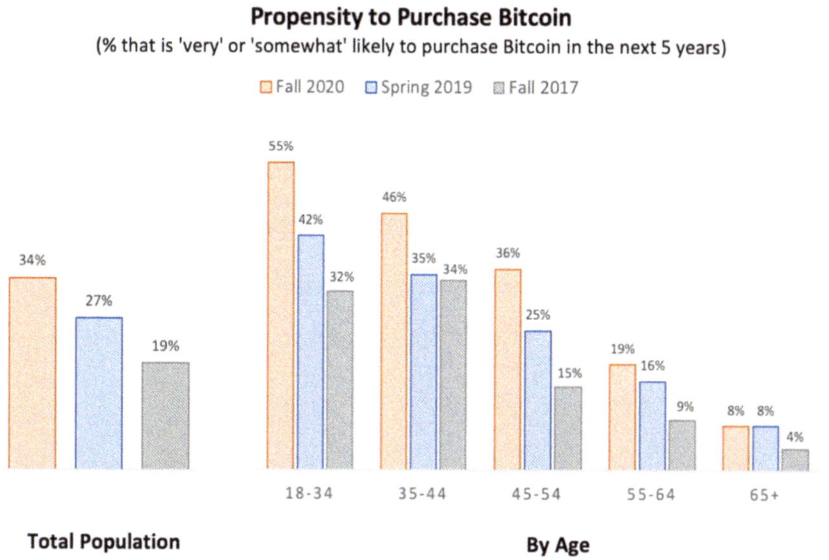

Fig. 10.22 Propensity to purchase Bitcoin

With an estimated $68 trillion in generational wealth expected to change hands over the next 25 years (including $48 trillion from the Baby Boomer generation), there is a possibility that more investments will be made in digital assets like Bitcoin and Ethereum in the future (Lee, 2021). So, it is safe to say that we are just at the beginning of the digital era.

References

Bogart, S. (2020). *Bitcoin is (Still) a demographic mega-trend: Data update - Blockchain Capital*. Blockchain Capital. https://blockchain.capital/bitcoin-is-still-a-demographic-mega-trend-data-update/.

Friesendorf, C., & Stern, J. (2020). Mangelnde Digitalisierung in der Finanzbranche. In *Digitalisierung des Auslandszahlungsverkehrs. essentials*. Springer. https://doi.org/10.1007/978-3-658-32738-5_1

Friesendorf, C., & Uedelhoven, L. (2021). Digital transformation of global mobility markets. In *Mobility in Germany. Springer briefs in business*. Springer. https://doi.org/10.1007/978-3-030-71849-7_1

Friesendorf, C., & Mir Haschemi, N. J. (2023). Private equity in Germany. In *Venture Capital for Digital Platform Start-ups. Springer business guides on the go*. Springer. https://doi.org/10.1007/978-3-031-33708-6

Lee, J. (2021). *The upcoming wealth transfer is about more than just money, it's about preference*. Edison Partners. https://www.edisonpartners.com/blog/yieldstreet/wealth/transfer/.

Miles, M. B., & Huberman, A. M. (1994). *Qualitative data analysis: An expanded sourcebook* (2nd ed.). Sage.

Petro, G. (2021). Gen Z is emerging as the sustainability generation. *Forbes*. https://www.forbes.com/sites/gregpetro/2021/04/30/gen-z-is-emerging-as-the-sustainability-generation/?sh=3b93aea38699

Saldaña, J. (2011). *Fundamentals of qualitative research*. Oxford University Press.

Sawyer, A. (2021). *How business and education can help Gen Z reframe the future | EY - Global*. EY. https://www.ey.com/en_gl/corporate-responsibility/how-business-and-education-can-help-gen-z-reframe-the-future.

Yamane, T., & Kaneko, S. (2021). Is the younger generation a driving force toward achieving the sustainable development goals? Survey experiments. *Journal of Cleaner Production, 292*. https://doi.org/10.1016/J.JCLEPRO.2021.125932

Chapter 11
Discussion and Conclusion

11.1 Learnings and Implications

By reviewing the literature and conducting an online survey on the banking industry in the process of writing this book, several learnings have been made. We will summarize key findings and implications in the upcoming sections of this chapter.

11.1.1 Transparency Builds Trust

From this research, it can be concluded that trust levels toward banks and financial service providers have declined in recent years. According to the Edelmann Trust Barometer, people from European countries trust banks less than people in other countries, which has been discussed in previous chapters. In the conducted online survey of this research, most respondents who were dissatisfied with their current bank would not recommend it to friends or family due to unclear or high-priced fees. The hidden costs associated with the bank's products and services are another reason why customers are dissatisfied. The implications that can be drawn from these learnings are that banks must increase their level of transparency in order to regain the trust of their clients. A manager or chief executive officer of a financial service institution must also take the lead in addressing societal challenges such as the impact of the Covid-19 pandemic, job automation, and sustainability (Edelman, 2021a, b). This requires an active internal communication with banking employees and dynamic outreach to external stakeholders using technological platforms or social media to understand stakeholder feedback, address problems, and communicate a strong will to be welfare-oriented.

C. Friesendorf, A. Blütener, *Decentralized Finance (DeFi)*, Business Guides on the Go, https://doi.org/10.1007/978-3-031-37488-3_11

11.1.2 Closing the Banking vs. Unbanked People Gap

It is also important to note that while big international investment banks such as the United States and China dominate the financial services industry by market capitalization (and other regional banks that provide a wide range of services and are well connected), banks are yet to reach a significant portion of the global population. As described in the previous chapters of the World Findex, there are currently over 1.7 billion people without access to financial services. The majority of these individuals reside in Asia, with the highest number of unbanked individuals found in China, Bangladesh, and Indonesia. From this, it can be concluded that there is a gap between banked and unbanked people that needs to be closed.

In some cases, banks are unable to reach the unbanked for a variety of reasons, including cultural differences, distance, or governance issues. There is an urgent need to close this gap so that everyone can have access to financial services that will create more transactions that is beneficial for banks, consumers, governments, and industry. An increase in the number of participants enables a diversity that helps make the financial services industry attractive in the offer of products and services, which further helps create an inclusive and fair environment.

Specifically, for this reason, decentralized finance (DeFi) could be a potential solution to this problem of a large gap of unbanked people. Unlike traditional banks that have physical outreach barriers, DeFi requires online access and thereby drastically fewer entry barriers to access banking services. In other words, by using the Internet, people who are unable to reach a bank because of its distance would be able to connect to the DeFi network and be able to conduct financial transactions through the network.

We purport that in the coming years, DeFi is going to be able to offer everything that a traditional bank is able to offer as well, including decentralized stablecoins, decentralized payment systems, decentralized derivatives, decentralized exchanges, decentralized lotteries, and decentralized wealth management.

11.1.3 ESG: Toward a Greener and Fairer World

The topic of sustainability or ESG—economic, social, and governance—in the financial sector is a major aspect of the book that was discussed in length. From the previous sections, several learnings and implications can be derived that should be taken into account. As a result of the online survey conducted by the bank, one of the most important findings was that most participants in the survey believe that their top management as well as the banks themselves are not doing enough to work toward a greener, fairer, and more transparent future.

Additionally, a large majority of participants believe that the most sustainable banks are online banks such as N26, Tomorrow, and DKB. According to this result, most people do not consider traditional banks that offer retail services to be sustainable at all. The reason for this is that the banks that provide retail services are usually large traditional banks such as Commerzbank, Deutsche Bank, or Sparkasse. Due to their size, these banks may be associated with low sustainability standards.

Since 2018, however, bigger banks have come under increasing pressure to comply with ESG goals. In recent years, global capital investments have increasingly focused on sustainability goals as well as environmental, social, and governance principles (ESG). Although ESG investing has grown rapidly worldwide, many issues remain for the financial industry since regulators and investors have not yet developed fully defined standards for ESG investing. However, regardless of the introduction of new policies in the coming months, financial institutions are already facing demands for more active ESG solutions from their stakeholders (institutional investors, rating agencies, customers), as EU authorities shape the new ESG regulatory framework.

As a result of this learning, financial institutions should consider how ESG goals affect their business model and core activities in order to map and prioritize the essential functions to be addressed (e.g., investment processes, product governance, risk controls) according to existing regulatory guidelines and market trends that are publicly available.

Younger generations, such as Generation Z, have also been found to have a higher risk appetite than older generations. According to the online survey conducted, participants from Generation Z are much more likely to invest in digital assets than their elders. Additionally, they are more likely to open up their own bank to promote a greener, more equitable, and more transparent future for the financial sector.

In contrast, Baby Boomers and Millennials tend to be more risk-averse. Digital assets are not favored by Baby Boomers, who prefer to invest in traditional investment products such as real estate, bonds, and shares. The millennial generation and Gen Z are much more familiar with digital assets, such as Bitcoin and NFTs, than previous generations. As a result of these learnings, it is clear that in the future, when generational wealth is changing and younger generations begin to inherit their parents' or grandparents' assets (which is estimated to be $68 trillion), DeFi will be able to continue to grow as younger generations will be more inclined to believe in digital assets and invest in them than older generations are.

11.1.4 Enhancing Digital Trust

The majority of participants who would open their own bank (mostly Gen Z and Millennials) would do so because they believe the current financial system is unjust. As a result of this finding, the previously mentioned lack of trust in traditional banks is further reinforced. For traditional banks to remain competitive in the future, they must regain the trust of their younger clients. As a result, there is a possibility that some other options, such as DeFi, will be able to outcompete them in the future.

DeFi offers many opportunities despite the challenges in the current environment of transition. Figure 11.1 illustrates these in a tabular form.

As a concept, DeFi has experienced rapid growth in the last few years. With digital assets receiving continuous media attention and interest from people across the globe, as well as from different demographics, it is also essential to evaluate some of the potential benefits and dangers related to this technology that may arise in the future.

11.1.5 DeFi Creates Low-Cost Entry

A major benefit that DeFi can offer is the ability to reduce transaction costs and friction for trading, settling, creating, and distributing financial assets by reducing transaction costs and friction. A simple example is circumventing intermediaries such as traditional banks in order to reduce the cost of loans for consumers since he does not have to pay the bank's transaction fees when he circumvents intermediaries. Customers can benefit greatly from DeFi as it has the potential to reduce the costs associated with trading, settling, creating, and distributing financial assets by removing friction in the trading, settling, creating, and distributing of financial assets through the removal of friction in terms of coordination between several parties, contracting, and technology as well as increasing transaction speed. In the next few years, this opportunity is expected to have a significant impact on a number of functions within today's securities and payments market infrastructure, such as RTGs, custody, FX services, clearinghouses, and secure messaging systems (Popa, 2022).

Opportunities and Challenges for DeFi

Opportunities	Challenges
Decreased transaction costs and friction for trading, settling, creating, and distributing financial assets	The high energy usage of the DLT leads to sustainability concerns
Easier market access	Regulatory concerns
Increase in functional interoperability	Constrained interoperability
Increased accountability	Inexperienced or small teams making immature governance decisions
Fostering a vibrant and active community of stakeholders in the network	Potential for financial crimes (e.g., money laundering)
Reduced counterparty risk and quicker settlements	Undeveloped or immature technology that is used for managing high-value digital assets. A poor design and implementation choices could lead to significant losses
Innovation without boundaries	Scalability and throughput of DLT could be limiting factors
Increased inclusivity of financial products and services	Short term investment returns
Increased stakeholder control	Possibility of disproportionate power for individual actors
Increased transparency and accountability in financial transactions	The high transparency in financial transactions could lead to privacy concerns

Fig. 11.1 Opportunities and challenges of DeFi

11.1.6 Need for Advanced DLT Solutions

DeFi faces a significant challenge when it comes to sustainability concerns. We live in an era where sustainability has become more and more important to customers and the government, which is why it has become necessary for companies to provide sustainable services to their customers. It is well known that digital ledger technologies (DLTs) are known for their high energy usage due to the proof-of-work verification method that is applied in these networks, which requires a large amount of processor power and electricity to operate.

According to experts, it is estimated that the Bitcoin network uses roughly 0.6% of the world's total electricity, which is quite inefficient (University of Cambridge, 2022). Although DLT is still in its infancy, it should not be overlooked when it comes to improving environmental sustainability goals in the future as a result of its infancy. In order to foster sustainability at scale, the technology itself needs to be further developed. As a result, regulators and policymakers must quickly adapt and develop regulations in order to spur the expansion of future energy systems while reducing the detrimental effects on the environment.

11.1.7 Increasing Financial Inclusiveness

A further opportunity that DeFi offers is the ability to make financial products and services more accessible to customers and increase the inclusiveness of financial products and services by providing easier market access. Due to DeFi's ability to provide products and services that are available 24/7 globally to anyone in the network, they have a great advantage over traditional banks in terms of the services and products they provide. In this way, customers can make transactions whenever they want to and they do not have to make an appointment with their financial advisor over the phone, for which they also have to pay a fee and also have to make an appointment in advance.

The opportunity to connect more of the unbanked people, who are currently numbering 1.7 billion worldwide, to financial services is also increased when barriers such as bank account requirements are removed. As another benefit, by operating fully online, DeFi enables people to access financial products and services from their own homes using a smartphone, tablet, or computer, from wherever they may be in the world.

11.1.8 Growth-Supportive Regulation

However, DeFi also has to face another very important challenge that it needs to overcome in order to succeed. It has already been mentioned in the previous chapters that the regulatory landscape of DeFi is not yet fully developed. There are still many regulatory questions that are still unanswered and enforcement challenges that need to be resolved when applying legal requirements to a global decentralized network. There is a need for regulators to think of regulations that also take into account the decentralized and automated nature of these systems when developing a regulatory framework. Aside from that, it is crucial for investors to inform themselves about the financial, compliance, and technological risks that could arise from an unregulated market as a result of unregulated markets. Lastly, another problem for DeFi is the extreme short-term return it is going to experience during its growth phase, which is going to change the expectations of users and could attract unethical actors.

11.1.9 Interoperability and Standardization

Achieving greater interoperability and standardization through DeFi will allow for the recomposition and reuse of financial primitives as a result of an increase in functional interoperability. Therefore, this is another opportunity for the technology to be used in the future. In spite of this, DeFi continues to face a challenge in terms of functional interoperability. Generally speaking, interoperability can be defined as the ability of two or more different systems to communicate with one another across different protocols (Boudjemaa, 2020).

Currently, in the traditional financial system, a lot of the payment infrastructure is interoperable. There is a good example of interoperability in the traditional financial system when people are able to swipe their credit cards in order to pay for a variety of different services and goods regardless of what currency is used to pay for them. When a person is traveling to a different country, they can be confident that their credit card will be able to be used for payments without having to worry about the different currency in the country that they are traveling to. This is particularly true when they are in a different country.

Interoperability occurs when different blockchains communicate with each other in order to exchange value. For example, when customers with Ethereum want to pay for their coffee at a coffee shop and realize that they didn't bring their wallet but are aware that the store also accepts bitcoins, they should be able to pay for their coffee in Ethereum. Ethereum's blockchain and Bitcoin's blockchain both need to be able to communicate with each other in order for them to work together.

Currently, this is not the case, however. For now, the technology is still in the process of being developed, and there are several workarounds that are already available in order to bypass the challenge of interoperability between blockchains that are already available. The downside of these, however, is that they make DeFi more centralized and therefore kill the idea and purpose of decentralization in the process. It is crucial for the DeFi space to find a way to resolve this problem and be able to establish cross-communication between blockchains; otherwise, the DeFi space will remain in its infancy as each blockchain has its own specific economy that is separate from the rest. In order to provide user-friendly products and services, it is essential to communicate across these silos so that they can interact with each other.

11.1.10 Increased Accountability in Decision-Making

With its software-based governance system, DeFi also provides the opportunity to increase the accountability for decisions made through its software-based governance process. However, when we take a close look at this opportunity, we know that there is a great risk of immature governance, which needs to be addressed as soon as possible. The risk of high-stake decisions being made within a network by an inexperienced or small team that does not have the necessary experience is a great one. As a result of the anonymity of the protocol developers, there is also a lack of accountability when it comes to the protocols. There is no doubt that a flawed protocol can pose a serious threat to a network, but being unable to hold the person accountable for their mistakes makes the situation even more dangerous. Unauthorized individuals may threaten the network with malicious code that may cause it to become unstable.

11.1.11 Diversity of Ideas and Creativity

Diversity contributes to the understanding of different perspectives and enhances creativity in networks. Having DeFi online provides a unique opportunity to attract people from around the world with diverse perspectives and backgrounds. Those who have access to the Internet are able to participate in these networks, which fosters an active and vibrant community of stakeholders. People who wish to harm others or use popular and vibrant networks for illegal purposes find the DeFi environment attractive for participation.

Since DeFi is not yet highly regulated and most parties are anonymous, it has the potential to facilitate financial crimes. A good example would be money laundering, which is already a serious threat to centralized cryptocurrency exchanges. As of 2021, cryptocurrency exchanges accounted for approximately 47% of all money laundering offenses (Sharma, 2022). The only requirements for cryptocurrency trading at the present time are the identification of customers and the registration of financial transactions. However, as long as DeFi is not adequately regulated, its platforms will be used for financial crimes such as money laundering or other questionable financial activities such as war financing.

11.1.12 Elimination of the Middleman

DeFi has the potential to increase settlement times by eliminating the middleman. In addition, capital can be freed up and counterparty risks can be reduced. With fewer intermediary layers, users are able to control their own assets, and smart contracts can even completely mitigate counterparty risk. These opportunities are created by removing intermediaries, such as banks, from transactions. When removing banks from a transaction, there are also risks and challenges to overcome. DeFi's technology has not yet been fully developed, and some functions are still in their infancy. If a user makes a mistake, such as transferring assets to the wrong address or network, there is no middleman such as a bank that can revert the smart contract and return the user's funds. As the technology is still in its infancy, faults may also occur. For example, smart contracts are executed by oracles that rely on information provided by data sources such as price feeds. In the event that oracles are compromised by malicious external attacks, the execution of the smart contract may be compromised. The removal of the intermediary therefore makes it necessary to find solutions to potential risks and challenges that need to be resolved to make the system safe and reliable for users.

11.1.13 Market Transition

Its open-source and permissionless nature offers DeFi the ability to explore and foster a new environment where developers are allowed to launch new and innovative financial applications much faster as they don't have to build core infrastructure or have to rely on permissioned and centralized financial services. Consequently, DeFi's environment requires constant innovation in order to retain its market share. However, the scalability and throughput of the DLT technology could be a substantial challenge for DeFi. A system's throughput is defined as the amount of transactions that can be processed by a given system over a particular period of time (Vigneri, 2022).

To achieve scalability in a DLT, it is necessary to overcome the blockchain trilemma, a term invented by Ethereum's founder Vitalik Buterin and consists of a triangle between decentralization, scalability, and security in which blockchains can only contribute to two of the three components. An example of this is the Bitcoin blockchain, which utilizes the proof-of-work (PoW) method. PoW requires a significant amount of energy to add a new block to the chain. Due to its high level of security and decentralization, Bitcoin's blockchain has a high level of security.

However, it sacrifices speed, which is a common problem with blockchains that needs to be resolved.

11.1.14 Ownership and Control

Another opportunity for DeFi is to increase stakeholder control significantly through its disintermediated and noncustodial service provision. By using decentralized finance, stakeholders have the opportunity to control their own assets and use them as they see fit. In most transactions, the intermediary holds the stakeholder's assets. The assets in the DeFi world are locked into smart contracts governed by boundaries that are selected by stakeholders themselves. In addition to keeping their assets in bank accounts, they may also hold their assets through noncustodial wallets. As a result, DeFi faces the challenge that there could be hidden centralization of authority within the network, which would give certain actors a disproportionate amount of power, thus undermining the principle of decentralization.

11.1.15 Auditability

One of the main objectives of DeFi's products and services is to make financial services more transparent. DeFi has a significant opportunity in this area. Traditional financial institutions are still not transparent enough, which is a crucial factor for users. In our survey, we could establish that most participants who were dissatisfied with their bank attributed their dissatisfaction to the unclear and hidden costs structure of their bank. Due to its blockchain-based records, DeFi offers greater transparency and auditability of transactions. However, there are still concerns regarding the privacy of DeFi's users. In the European Union, where data privacy is a strictly and heavily regulated issue, privacy considerations may become in conflict with the transparency of the transaction offered.

11.2 Strategic Agility: Incumbent Positioning of Banks

In this section, we examine the options for banks to regain their influence and market share among various stakeholders in a fast-moving world of digitalization, digital assets, and digital business models. Moreover, we will provide an in-depth examination of strategic agility and other digital business models, including digital asset management, that is becoming an integral component of strategic and operational decision-making in the future.

11.2.1 Operational Versus Strategic Agility

Theoretically speaking, there are two types of agility covered extensively in management literature. These are, namely, operational agility and strategic agility. Operational agility refers to improving an existing product catering to a specific target group of customers, while strategic agility refers to creating a new market with new products that will reach new consumers. In our study, we note that banks are more focused on the operational agility aspects of catering to their most loyal customers, which is, from the management perspective, the right step. However, the current digital transformation of finance and the evolving market for new financial needs and means require bankers and managers to wear the strategic agility hat to respond to the emergent new segment. This means that incumbent banks must be operationally and strategically agile. Also, organizational agility is necessary to enable strategic agility (Denning, 2018).

11.2.2 Internal Change Management

Many banks and financial institutions are recognizing the importance of strategic agility. Specifically, the presence of big tech companies and fintechs put much pressure on banks in Germany to reevaluate their business models. For mid-level and senior managers, the objective should be to maintain a strategic focus and direction while still being able to adjust to short-term changes in the market environment. To achieve such agility or flexibility, the organization and its decision-making process must make a great deal of effort firstly in understanding the development of new technologies, new business models as established by local fintechs, capture the potential of ESG elements, and finally to develop within the team new products that attract existent and new customers.

This systematic approach makes it possible for banks to consider new digital products and new markets in a fast-moving world. Banks and banking professionals are aware of the pace of digitalization, but in order sustain market share, they need to develop concerted efforts within the banks that will set the speed for an internal change management or transition process to tackle the competitive pressure in the larger banking market, both locally and internationally.

11.2.3 Digital Portfolio in Wealth Products

Digital assets in wealth management, such as non-fungible tokens (NFTs), could be a possible new digital business model for banks. NFTs are currently experiencing a great deal of hype, especially in regard to investments in gaming and art. Since banks typically offer their wealthy clients all kinds of investment options, such as real estate, art, stocks, and bonds, they should also consider offering NFTs and other digital assets. As a result, they will be able to attract new customers in addition to their existing customers, as well as not miss out on the revenue that could be generated by offering new and existing customers digital assets.

People will always be unwilling to take the risk of managing their own assets, even though DeFi would give them full control over their assets. It is possible that some individuals are not interested in full control. Banks will have another opportunity to manage these assets on behalf of their clients. A bank could, for example, offer a wallet or vault for digital assets similar to how people have their normal bank accounts. The lack of regulations and the anonymous environment in which digital assets are traded will present a challenge for banks when offering digital assets (especially cryptocurrencies).

Onboarding new customers usually involves a great deal of compliance on the part of the bank. To properly onboard a client, a bank must conduct background checks such as KYC (Know Your Customer), which could pose a major challenge for banks when implementing a similar system for digital assets. Decentralization aims to remove such barriers and make financial services more accessible to everyone. Consequently, if banks fail to find a way to work effectively with the concept of decentralization, they will be left behind.

11.2.4 Digital Identity Products as an Opportunity

A new area of digital business that has the potential to become a big new business for traditional banks is the area of digital identity or digital ID, which is another new digital business field. A number of disruptive and innovative new services and products have been launched in the last few years, which makes it increasingly difficult for banks to verify that the employees and customers they claim to be are who they claim to be. As more and more financial products and services are becoming more and more digitized, banks have to develop new tools and methods to prevent fraud and determine the identity of the people they are dealing with.

The cybercrime industry has been flourishing for the past three years, especially since the pandemic started, as people are now spending more time at home, shopping online, and spending more time on the Internet in general because of the pandemic. According to the Theft Resource Center (ITRC), there had been a spike in cybercrime and companies experiencing data breaches by 17% in 2021 (Waqas, 2022). Identity theft is one of the most common types of cybercrime. In addition to cybercrime, financial institutions have also seen a spike in the legitimate use of digital products and services among their customer base over the past few years (Camplisson, 2022).

The banks have access to a rich pool of verified identities of people with bank accounts that they have access to. Anyone who uses a checking account must authenticate themselves before they can use it. The banks, as regulated financial service providers, are also legally required to verify the identities of their customers in order to provide them with financial services. Some countries, such as Sweden, Denmark, and Estonia, are already further ahead and demonstrate how data can be used for new solutions with digital identities for e-commerce as well as for official processes. The banking industry is also still considered to be a reliable one when it comes to the issue of confidentiality.

The central provision and management of digital identities by banks would solve a lot of problems in the long run. In studies that have been conducted in the EU, it has been found that every EU citizen has almost a hundred digital access data for online shops, social media accounts, or email accounts. It is widely believed that the potential of central digital identities, such as those offered by government solutions such as the electronic ID card, is being met with widespread skepticism (Axians, 2021). In order to fill the trust gap that is left in the state, banks clearly have an opportunity to use their resources and know-how to be the first mover and innovation agent in creating verifiable digital identities and thereby directly address the topic of financial crime.

11.3 Recent Developments and Future Outlook

From our study, we conclude that the future looks promising for decentralized finance (DeFi) products and services, given the emergence of new technologies, ease of setting up companies of varying sizes locally and internationally, and the growing interest of the media and investors that is reflective of flood of information of this topic among households and companies. It is worth mentioning that as a result of recent developments, there are five main DeFi trends emerging that we believe to be areas of opportunity for investment in the upcoming years. The following are some of the trends that we are experiencing in the scientific and practitioner worlds:

DeFi Key Trends

The traditional financial services and products will be incorporated into the DeFi environment in the near future.

DeFi will be a field exploring various product models that enables monetizing blockchain gaming.

DeFi aims to solve scalability problems by implementing cross-chain technology.

Automated market makers (AMM) and decentralized exchanges (DEXs) are expected to drive DeFi growth.

The importance of governance tokens is expected to increase in the future (Howarth, 2022).

It is anticipated that in the coming months and years, more and more traditional financial products will be subjected to enter the DeFi environment. One of the prime examples of this is the derivatives market, which is estimated to be ten times larger than the global GDP as it stands today. While on the other hand, there is still a lot of immaturity in the DeFi derivatives market at the moment. DeFi derivatives are dominated by a platform called dYdX, which accounts for approximately 40% of the market.

In addition to derivatives, Wrapped Bitcoin (WBTC) is another way that derivatives can be used to grow the DeFi market. There are several ways in which WBTC can be used to create a derivative of Bitcoin that is based on Ethereum. As a result, Bitcoin owners will have the option to farm, lend, or stake their coins on the Ethereum network in this way.

In addition to traditional financing instruments, such as options contracts, the DeFi industry is also seeing an increase in its use. A DeFi marketplace for option contracts is called Hegic, and users are able to enter into option contracts for Bitcoin and Ether on the platform. The total combined trading volume of Bitcoin and Ether option contracts will reach around 9.2 billion USD daily (Howarth, 2022) by the end of 2023, according to Hegic.

There is a prediction that monetized blockchain gaming will be the next DeFi trend that will come in the next few years. Currently, there are more than two billion gamers in the world who spend approximately 159 billion USD every year on gaming (Krion, 2021). In the next eight years, that number is predicted to rise to approximately 256 billion USD (Financial News Media, 2020).

Currently, with more and more people dedicating a large part of their income and time to this type of entertainment, both creators and players want to increase the monetization of the video game industry in order to continue to grow. There is a way to monetize the gaming industry through the use of blockchain technology. The creators and developers of the games are transferring them to blockchains instead of playing them on consoles such as the Playstation or Xbox. As a result, the games can no longer be played on a central server but on a blockchain instead. By completing certain tasks in the game, players are then able to earn tokens by completing certain tasks within the game. By doing this, people are able to earn money while playing games, which is a big motivation for most people to keep playing these games.

To transfer these assets, however, DeFi protocols will have to be used. Ubisoft developed one of the first blockchain games, HashCraft, in 2019, which led to the development of a number of other games over the past few years. It was announced in 2020 that cryptocurrency owners would be able to stake and sponsor professional games and tournaments through BitSport. It has now been announced that Crypto.com, a large cryptocurrency platform, is going to be one of the official sponsors of the FIFA world cup in Qatar in 2022. Therefore, it can be said that digital assets will continue to exert a great deal of influence in the upcoming months and years, which is to be expected.

Thirdly, one of the future trends of DeFi is the introduction of cross-chain technology, which will drastically improve the scalability of blockchains in the future.

There are some technology problems with the scalability of the DeFi products that are limiting their use and their growth in the future. Nevertheless, cross-chain technology will enable smart contracts and transactions to cross from one blockchain to another. Consequently, interoperability will make it easier for DeFi platforms to scale than they do on the Ethereum blockchain alone.

Fourthly, Automated Market Makers (AMMs) and Decentralized Exchanges (DEXs) are expected to fuel the growth of DeFi. In the DeFi space, one of the main challenges is balancing decentralization and efficiency. Coinbase, for example, is a cryptocurrency platform that facilitates quick and easy transactions. As a public company, Coinbase lacks decentralization. By combining decentralization and efficiency through the use of AMMs, DEX is expected to grow even more rapidly. A DEX was able to surpass trading volumes of 120 billion USD in 2021, and as more people move away from centralized platforms such as Coinbase to decentralized markets, the volume of trades will increase further (Howarth, 2022).

Last but not least, governance tokens will become increasingly important in the future. Every blockchain issues its own tokens, which confer voting rights on their owners. In parallel with the growth of the blockchain, the value of governance tokens is also increasing. As the DeFi industry evolves, people, institutions, and investors are going to become increasingly interested in shaping the future of the network.

As DeFi continues to grow, there will be even more trends emerging that will be of interest to consumers. DeFi is poised to play a significant role in the digital age that is just beginning. As a result of the digital financial revolution, traditional centralized financial institutions will have to develop strategies to attract new customers and new markets in order to maintain their market share.

11.4 Conclusion

This book investigates the possibility of decentralized finance (DeFi) disrupting traditional institutionalized banking and its worldwide use-cases using the research methods: namely, literature reviews on traditional and digital products and a survey that was conducted online. As a result of our research, we found that trust levels among the general public toward financial service providers such as banks and insurance companies have decreased over the past few years, particularly during the Covid-19 pandemic. Europe is the region in which trust levels have declined the most, including countries like Italy, Spain, and Germany, which are all part of the European Union. Additionally, as a result of our research, we have learned that there are currently over 1.7 billion unbanked people who do not have access to financial services for a range of reasons, including cultural issues, distance, governance, and demographic issues.

In order to open a bank account, private persons and companies have to overcome numerous hurdles that make it difficult for them to do so. There are many regulations and rules that must be followed in order to be eligible to open an account with a bank due to the centralization of banks. In addition, financial institutions are required to conduct a thorough background check in order to onboard a new client who wishes to take out a loan, a process known as KYC (Know Your Customer). In addition to these regulations, there are many other reasons why financial services are not available to everyone.

There is a huge gap between those who are banked and those who are unbanked, and it is only going to get larger as time goes by. There is therefore a need to find a way to make financial services more accessible and more equitable to the global population, which is why it is necessary to find robust yet agile solutions. In our analyses, we deem that there are many opportunities and solutions in the evolving field of DeFi. It is due to the fact that DeFi's technology is based on the Internet that it is able to connect the unbanked with financial services as a result of its technology. As long as you own a computer, smartphone, or tablet and have access to the Internet, you are able to participate in the network and use DeFi's services and products.

As we see it, DeFi is capable of transforming the financial sector because it will increase the transparency of financial services and transactions as a result of its auditable and transparent ecosystem, which is designed to increase the safety and security of transactions. As previously mentioned, it will also increase the accessibility of financial services since people will be able to access DeFi applications without having to worry about discrimination due to their geographical status, gender, nationality, race, or beliefs, as well as the lack of a fear of discrimination based on that status.

Moreover, DeFi is going to be able to increase the efficiency of financial transactions due to the fact that the programmable money will eliminate the need for centralized intermediaries (banks or insurance companies), which will lead to a more efficient and affordable financial market as a result of the programmable money. The final benefit of DeFi is that it makes finance convenient for its customers. The users of DeFi are able to send their money anywhere at any time to any other user who has access to digital assets via wallets for as little as a few minutes in exchange for a small fee and only a small amount of waiting time.

In addition to everything that was described above, it has already been made possible for DeFi users to undertake the following functions, as seen in the box below.

DeFi Users Can:

Take out loans without having to fill out huge amounts of paperwork and repay your debts whenever you want.

You will be able to earn yields on unproductive assets without being locked into a lock-in/maturity period.

Execute their automated trading strategies in a timely manner.

Despite all these opportunities and advancements, DeFi remains an active and growing field. It still faces a number of challenges, notwithstanding the opportunities.

There are several vulnerabilities with the technology behind DeFi that can be attributed to liquidity mismatches, a lack of shock-absorbing capacity, high leverage, and its built-in interconnectedness. In order for DeFi to become widely accepted as a financial transaction intermediary, several conditions must be met, for example, appropriate regulation and improved scalability of tokenization and blockchain technology. As a result, it is essential that regulators consider a regulation system that also takes into account the fact that these systems are decentralized and automated. In addition to that, it is crucial for investors to inform themselves about the financial, compliance, and technological risks that could arise when dealing with an unregulated market.

In light of our extensive research into the matter, we believe that DeFi is going to disrupt institutionalized banking in the near future. It is obvious from the results of the online survey that especially the younger generations who are increasingly concerned about sustainability have already invested heavily in technology, according to the results of the survey. It is estimated that there will be a transfer of \$68 trillion worth of generational wealth over the next 25 years (including \$48 trillion from the Baby Boomer generation), resulting in more investment in digital assets, such as Bitcoin and Ethereum. Aside from that, we also believe that the symbiosis between ESG and DeFi could have a huge impact on the financial industry since it is important to younger generations that sustainability is considered. Consequently, there is going to be a premium price paid by market participants for companies and systems that are able to provide benefits to society as a whole.

Accordingly, one could say that banks are going to have to adapt and further push the digitalization of their products and services in the near future in order to remain competitive and maintain their market shares in the near future. The CEOs and top managers of the companies will have to find a way of maintaining sustainability as one of their top priorities while building new markets to attract new customers at the same time. For banks, strategic agility will be one of the most important aspects of their operations. Otherwise, they will lose their customer base in the future. New digital business models, such as digital asset management, have been proposed in this book because there will always be people who trust their banks with their financial assets. In this manner, banks will be able to stay up to date with technology and its newest trends. In conclusion, we can say that the digital age is still in its infancy. Several trends and developments are predicted to enter the market in the next few years in favor of blockchain technology, and we should be prepared to welcome DeFi and the future of finance.

References

Axians. (2021). *Digital identity is becoming a business model of the future for banks*. Digital Chiefs. https://www.digital-chiefs.de/digitale-identitaet-banken-geschaeftsmodell-der-zukunft/

Boudjemaa, A. (2020). *Cross-chain interoperability: Enabling the future of DeFi | HackerNoon*. Hackernoon. https://hackernoon.com/cross-chain-interoperability-enabling-the-future-of-defi-7et3wgr

Camplisson, L. (2022). *Every bank's 2022 resolution should be digital identity - Future identity*. Future Identity. https://thefutureidentity.com/every-banks-2022-resolution-should-be-digital-identity/

Denning, S. (2018). *What is strategic agility?* Forbes https://www.forbes.com/sites/stevedenning/2018/01/28/what-is-strategic-agility/?sh=3fab85b8a0b1.

Edelman. (2021a). *Edelman Trust Barometer 2021*. In Edelman Barometer. https://www.edelman.com/sites/g/files/aatuss191/files/2021-03/2021 Edelman Trust Barometer.pdf

Edelman. (2021b). *Edelman Trust Barometer 2021 Technology Sector*. Edelman. https://www.edelman.com/sites/g/files/aatuss191/files/2021-03/2021 Edelman Trust Barometer Tech Sector Report_0.pdf

Financial News Media. (2020). *Global gaming market expected to exceed $256 billion by 2025*. PR News Wire. https://www.prnewswire.com/news-releases/global-gaming-market-expected-to-exceed-256-billion-by-2025-301182238.html

Howarth, J. (2022). *Top 5 DeFi trends for 2022-2024. Exploding Topics*. https://explodingtopics.com/blog/defi-trends.

Krion, A. (2021). *The DeFi boom is finally here, and blockchain gaming will reap the rewards | Nasdaq*. Nasdaq. https://www.nasdaq.com/articles/the-defi-boom-is-finally-here-and-blockchain-gaming-will-reap-the-rewards-2021-02-22

Popa, A. (2022). *The opportunities of DeFi for the financial sector explained – The Paypers*. The Paypers. https://thepaypers.com/expert-opinion/the-opportunities-of-defi-for-the-.

Sharma, R. (2022). *Use of DeFi protocols for money laundering grew in 2021*. Investopedia. https://www.investopedia.com/use-of-defi-protocols-for-money-laundering-5217387

University of Cambridge. (2022). *Cambridge Bitcoin Electricity Consumption Index (CBECI)*. Cambridge Centre for Alternative Finance. https://ccaf.io/cbeci/index

Vigneri, L. (2022). *Sharding: Throughput, scalability and why we need them*. IOTA Blog. https://blog.iota.org/sharding-throughput-scalability-and-why-we-need-them/

Waqas. (2022). *Identity theft statistics you need to know in 2022*. Hackread. https://www.hackread.com/identity-theft-statistics-you-need-know-in-2022/

MIX
Papier aus verantwortungsvollen Quellen
Paper from responsible sources
FSC® C105338

If you have any concerns about our products,
you can contact us on
ProductSafety@springernature.com

In case Publisher is established outside the EU,
the EU authorized representative is:
Springer Nature Customer Service Center GmbH
Europaplatz 3, 69115 Heidelberg, Germany

Printed by Libri Plureos GmbH
in Hamburg, Germany